Never
BETTER

To Dr mogri

Thank you for taking
good care of us!

Cal

never better
on 5/20/11

Never BETTER

How Legionnaire's Disease Gave Meaning to My Life

CALVIN L. KING

iUniverse, Inc.
New York Bloomington

Never Better
How Legionnaire's Disease Gave Meaning to My Life

iUniverse books may be ordered through booksellers or by contacting:

iUniverse
1663 Liberty Drive
Bloomington, IN 47403
www.iuniverse.com
1-800-Authors (1-800-288-4677)

ISBN: 978-1-4502-5358-1 (pbk)
ISBN: 978-1-4502-5359-8 (cloth)
ISBN: 978-1-4502-5360-4 (ebk)

Library of Congress Control Number: 2010912562

Printed in the United States of America

iUniverse rev. date: 8/25/2010

To my family and friends, relax and embrace life to the fullest.

Contents

Acknowledgments

I gratefully acknowledge my family for their support of this project. From the time I was a small boy, occasionally my mother shared the history of my grandparents with me. Those accounts had more significance than ever as I began this work. The object lessons my parents taught me also helped me clearly understand the genesis of my dogged determination. My brother Rod read drafts, listened to ideas, and provided some details of the events during the darkest days of my illness. He has been my best friend and close adviser. I'm thankful to my wife Michele, who encouraged me to write and exercised patience with me during the entire process.

Many thanks go to my colleague Joni Solano. She spent countless hours proofreading drafts of the manuscript, providing candid feedback, and instructing me on the elements of writing style. Her mentorship was invaluable. I'm also indebted to a circle of friends who read the early versions and shared their thoughts about this story.

Preface

On a Saturday night in March 2009, my wife Michele and I attended worship service at our church, Lakewood Church in Houston, Texas. Lakewood is one of the largest places of worship in America. Literally thousands of people attend each service. That night was no exception. We sat in the rear of the colossal sanctuary, intently watching Pastor Joel Osteen on the Jumbotron perched high above the main floor. As is the norm, Joel preached an encouraging and inspiring sermon. During the speech he said, "Some of you have been called to write a book." Michele and I stole a quick glance at each other. At that moment, we both felt Pastor Joel had spoken directly to me. I had a one-of-a-kind account of triumph to tell, but until then, I hadn't felt compelled to share the story by way of a book.

During the first week of August 2000, my life took a dramatic change. I had charm, a body chiseled by rigorous workouts, and a successful career as a financial service executive when, during a business trip, I contracted Legionnaire's disease. This obscure sickness was caused by bacteria that led to acute respiratory infection. The result was life-threatening pneumonia and other serious complications. Within a few dreadful days, I narrowly escaped death and lost the ability to speak plainly as a result of dysarthria, one of the conditions caused by the rare disease.

The *Legionella* bacteria wreaked absolute havoc on my body. In addition to speech impairment and diminished lung capacity, the encounter with Legionnaire's caused swelling of my cerebellum. This enlargement of a critical area of the brain triggered by very high and persistent fever left me with damaged motor skills (a condition called ataxia). The ataxia affected my eye-hand coordination, and affected my ambulatory functions. I had been an avid runner and cyclist for years. I wondered if I'd ever race again.

During the years that followed, Michele, my family and friends, had a front-row seat to witness my long struggle to recover from the aftereffects of Legionnaire's disease. From time to time, during my recovery, I relearned simple activities most people take for granted, such as chewing gum, buttoning my shirt with ease, or drinking without a straw. Michele would celebrate each victory with me. On several occasions, she suggested I write a book to help others understand the importance of faith, perseverance, and bravery, the revelation of a man destined to overcome nearly insurmountable odds to find new meaning in life.

Pastor Joel's words resonated with Michele. The next morning, she urgently persuaded me the time had come to start the project. Her passion was the impetus that started the wave of inertia I rode until I completed the project. *Never Better* tells the story of my battle to overcome the personal anguish of speech impairment, weakened body, and depression that threatened to consume my whole life. It is the story of my single-minded determination to learn to speak and resume a career as a successful call center executive. However, there is much more to the story.

When I telephoned a friend to share that I was about to publish a book about surviving Legionnaire's disease, I thought I heard a yawn on the other end of the line! She said, "Cal, I've heard the story of someone overcoming an illness a million times. What makes this any different? What's the real lesson here?" I agreed with her. The truly hot topics today are about celebrities and their foibles, although every week there is a news magazine feature about some brave American who has looked death squarely in the eye, survived, and gone on to do great things. Most people enjoy feel-good stories, but at the risk of sounding glib, that theme doesn't "sell" as briskly as it used to. My friend's questions reminded me of something I already knew. My life wasn't solely defined by being stricken by or overcoming a rare disease. The years prior to that fateful episode had also been full of unique adventures and learning experiences that shaped my life and would help others.

During my search for a literary professional to represent me for this project, I read an agent's description of her published authors. Each had one or more of the following qualifications: an immigrant parent, an alcoholic parent, divorced parents, abusive parents, a parent with mental illness, or a parent who died tragically. In addition, they were members of one or more of the following groups: adopted children, gays, Jews, blacks, Texans, academics, Mormons, or immigrants writing English as a second language. As I read the characteristics, I thought, *that's me*, a black, Texan, corporate executive with divorced parents. Many of my life events related to some of those attributes fashioned my thinking. I wrote about those memories in this book. These episodes, along with my faith, gave me the strength to go on with my life after nearly dying. Many other people in the same predicament would have thrown in the towel.

Life moves at a breakneck pace with events, change, and decisions happening in an instant. Most of us grant precious little time for tolerating others who don't fit a perfect mold. One of the doctors who treated me told me flatly, "You know, people are so mean. They won't understand all you've been through." I didn't believe him. Over the preceding twenty years, I'd enjoyed an uncanny string of successes. I expected it would only be a matter of time before I managed my own company. Surely, I wouldn't have to worry about how people would perceive me with my newly acquired disabilities. A big surprise awaited me. I had been as guilty as the next person of living a microwave life. Until the watershed event of August 2000 thrust a new outlook upon me, I had no clue what people with special needs or physical impairment faced. I learned they endure secret anguish, caused by hurtful stares and discrimination from "normal" people every day of their lives.

Before getting sick, my extroverted persona exuded confidence and featured a magnetism that captured the attention of friends and strangers. Afterwards, I was uncoordinated, skinny, and I talked funny. Though my thoughts were lucid and my mind worked with agility, I could only speak one slurred syllable at a time—and only with great effort. To make matters worse, I drooled uncontrollably. As a result, people frequently dismissed me as hearing-impaired, or worse yet, mentally challenged. My pride and feelings were crushed whenever this happened. I became an introvert in order to avoid the pain of rejection. I lived a personal hell no one else could fully understand and learned a secret anguish of the disabled.

When tragedy befalls us, invariably we ask a simple question. Why? I asked this simple question a thousand times after August 2000. Why did I contract this terrible disease? Why is one person subjected to affliction, discomfort, or calamity while another is spared? Many people grapple with these questions. Few, if any, find any answers. In the role of corporate executive, I'd been trained to understand the reasoning behind business decisions. Usually, after some thought, research, or perhaps listening to presentations, the answers came easily. This situation represented a whole new ballgame altogether. It tested my mind and faith in God unlike any other problem I had ever encountered.

Some misguided and overzealous Christians bury the wounded in spirit. A Christian friend told me I got sick as punishment for sin in my life. I had grown up in the Baptist church and been a person of faith. I read and committed scriptures to memory. No one knew better than me that I had not achieved perfection. Parts of my life were a total mess. I had an ex-wife and estranged children to prove the point. Nevertheless, my personal belief system wouldn't let me accept God had punished me by sentencing me to a disease that left me broken and depressed. It wasn't the answer I sought. I simply didn't believe God was some cosmic boogeyman who cast a sickness upon me because I had been a cad. I've since forgiven that person, but I've never agreed to meet with him again.

I can't say that I'll ever truly know the answers to my questions, but I've found meaning in my life. I'm pleased to know sharing my story will give someone hope and belief in the ability to overcome fear and obstacles in his life. Although it has been scary to pull the covers off my deepest thoughts, I'm humbled and honored to know sharing those candid reflections inspires and encourages others. My personal reward, achieved by virtue of writing this book, has been a cleansing of my mind and soul.

I didn't feel cleansed and peaceful overnight. It required a journey. People have their own ideas about how one settles upon a specific life course. Some think events are determined by serendipity, others believe it is karma, still others ascribe to the theory of self-driven destiny. I respect the beliefs of others, but I believe our lives are divinely ordered.

My childhood years were spent in a northern Indiana town during Lyndon Johnson's Great Society. Thanks to President Johnson's social programs and the Civil Rights movement of the 1960s, I attended desegregated schools and lived in a racially mixed neighborhood. Even though I never lost the colloquialisms or dialect of my race, I listened closely and mimicked the way the white kids in my neighborhood spoke. I worked hard to toggle between two cultures. I didn't want to be called an Uncle Tom by my black friends; however, I found myself very intrigued with white friends. I walked down an unusual path.

Looking back now, I realize divine destiny enabled me to meet the CEO of a large company, who recommended me for a management training job at one of the largest banks in Indiana. His referral came in spite of the fact that I hadn't yet finished college and had no prior training in financial services. I smiled and confidently exchanged pleasantries with him and his colleagues, in their dialect, on the days they came into a restaurant in which I worked as an assistant manager. After several such interactions, the CEO pulled me aside and quietly said, "I know someone looking for someone like you." He sat on the bank board of directors, so I already had the job. Within three years of the referral, I became the first African American officer of the company. I enjoyed a life of acclaim and respect in my small community.

Pastor Joel said something else that March evening. "God has one person that will look favorably upon you. That person will work on your behalf, and your life will never be the same." I thought he was making a prediction about what would happen during the process of writing and publishing this book. I realize now, Joel's profession also applied to what happened to me thirty years ago with the CEO.

Ultimately, that first banking role led to a steady climb up the corporate ladder of large financial institutions. Along the way, I developed relationships that touched or reshaped my life. I discussed many of those relationships in this book. A few of the names were changed for confidentiality sake. The trip of destiny continued when I accepted a role running a large call center in Houston, shortly after the Y2K scare ended. Eight months later, while in Chicago for a business conference, I inhaled aerosols containing the *Legionella* bacteria. The bug found a respite deep inside my lungs. My life's path took a turn I never saw coming.

Part I
LIVING DREAMS

Chapter 1
LOOKING FOR SOMEONE LIKE YOU

The Chance Meeting That Changed My Life

THE FACES OF THE SENIOR EXECUTIVES were stoic as I walked to the platform in the mahogany-paneled board room. Fortunately, the new gray pin-striped suit fit my tall frame perfectly and hid the involuntary trembling. I clutched the podium with glistening palms, stared down at the freshly shined Bostonians, and squarely positioned my hands to steady myself. This was it; the career-changing moment I'd prepared for. I had rehearsed the talking points ten times in front of the bathroom mirror the previous night. Thank goodness for spotting my boss in the back of the room. Her wink calmed me and prompted a smile in return. I could do this.

Just as I began the opening remarks, the unthinkable happened. A mysterious, invisible force swooped down, slapped my mouth shut and slammed me to the floor. The stunned executives gasped. Two of them rushed to the podium. When the first one reached me, I sat straight up in bed. My nightshirt, pillow case, and sheets were drenched in sweat, and my heart pounded. *Why do I have this strange dream nearly every night, and relive it during the day when my mind idles? I have to get some sleep. Tomorrow could be the beginning of something big.*

* * * *

Stepping out of the artificial warmth of the Ford SUV into the powerful northeastern Indiana wind of early January snapped me awake from the bizarre daydream. A bitter cold gale whistled loudly in my face and pelted me with a stinging snow. "The Hawk," the name my friends and I called the intolerable wintry conditions, showed no signs of mercy in the foreseeable future. The bone numbing wind chill of minus ten degrees and the accompanying ten inches of snow plowed neatly around the iced over asphalt airport parking lot made me realize this day would be far better spent staying inside reading Stephen Covey, Max Depree or Tom Peters to learn the fine art of leadership.

As I trekked the half mile through icy gray mush from my parking space to the airport terminal to catch the early morning flight, I cursed myself for living in a glacier all these years. I really hated winter in the Midwest and had made a promise to myself nearly every year; one day I would move to the Sunbelt where there was no biting wind, ice, or snow. After pushing down the narrow aisle and plopping down into the window seat, I caught a glimpse of bundled-up airline workers de-icing the sprawling jet wings. Why hadn't I been brave enough to make the move to a place of perpetual warmth? After all, the firstborn prince of the King family should experience the best life the world had to offer.

Y2K had just come and gone. Amazingly, the world hadn't ended as so many scholars boldly predicted. Jesus had not made his much-anticipated triumphant, New Millennium return delivering me and other believers into heavenly bliss. The Federal Reserve hadn't crashed, and computers around the globe continued to hum along, never giving a second thought to the talk about the catastrophic events and unbridled mayhem that was surely the destiny of all the earth. Now that the New Millennial scare had passed, the time had come to migrate south.

Though I had traveled to virtually every major city east of the Mississippi, I'd never been to Houston. I never had a reason to. The only things I thought Houston had to offer were cowboys, tumbleweed, and George H. W. Bush. None of that interested me. The highlight of this trip would be seeing my old friend and colleague, Kathleen, who said she needed me to manage one of the departments in her operation at a Houston based corporation. I would love to work with her again but couldn't purge my mind of the thought that this trip could end up being nothing more than an obligatory jaunt.

My interest had been aroused true enough, but surely I didn't have the courage to leave northeast Indiana where things had gone so well and life moved at a comfortable midwestern pace. It would take inertia to make a step like this and I was stuck not really going anywhere to speak of lately. And yet, my pulse quickened with the idea of doing something daring. I had no idea relocating to this faraway city would shock my tranquil world and bring me face-to-face with an enemy that would change my life forever.

As I settled in during the flight it occurred to me that this trip really began more than twenty years back on another cold gray northeastern Indiana winter day between Christmas and New Year's. That day found me like virtually every other, working full-time at Lucky Steer Steak House. As the youngest manager in the chain, clearly my destiny was a career of managing restaurants. I had started there five years earlier while in high school, cooking steak and comforting customers with coffee refills. My loving parents, Doc and Pops's long marriage was in shambles by then but not before both pounded life lessons into my very being.

Doc started sharing the stories of her father, James "Price" Love, my Gramps, when I reached the age of five or six years old. Gramps owned the black barber shop, restaurant, and taxi service in Frenchmans Bayou, Arkansas, roughly thirty miles north of Memphis along the famous Highway 61 blues corridor. Price sharecropped on the J. M. Speck Plantation and partnered in business with the Speck family. He further supplemented his income by helping the Specks run the local liquor store and selling hot cooked meals from its storefront.

Doc drilled into my head all the stories that demonstrated Price's work ethic and resourcefulness. He saved his cash and took care of the entire extended Love family. That included not only his sisters but my uncles, who worked in the family farming business as soon as they turned thirteen. Doc had a credo: *By God, if my brothers started working when they were thirteen, so would I.*

Price's beloved baby daughter, Cora Lee, married Lenwood "Sonny" King, the son of a dirt-poor sharecropper. The King family lived a few miles away in a rundown shack in Turrell, Arkansas. Cora had barely turned sixteen years old when they jumped the broom of matrimony. Even though they were both young, they committed themselves to the goal of rearing their children to work hard and become self-reliant. Their children would not be sharecroppers.

The newlyweds left Arkansas in 1956 and moved north to Fort Wayne, Indiana, to be near my Pops's mother, Sarah West. More importantly, they wanted to get away from the Speck men, who had a reputation of fondling the black women of Frenchmans Bayou. One of the young Speck boys spent virtually every day at Price's house. His intentions weren't good at all nor were those of his brother, whom everyone called "Rat." Ironically, my grandmother, Lucille, was the caregiver for Rat Speck's family.

While the Specks were allegedly ogling the black women, they would not tolerate a black man contemplating anything with their women. My uncle Ted had a wandering eye for one of the white girls. Rat Speck told Ted in no uncertain terms that if he caught him looking at his daughter again, he would kill him. It was no joke. The twisted rules of segregation were alive and well in Frenchmans Bayou just as they were across the rest of the South.

A few months after settling down in Indiana, my parents returned to Arkansas for a visit with me in tow. I had inherited the very light-skinned complexion of my mother. This proved to be a dangerous thing in 1950s Arkansas. Word had gotten back to Price that the locals were angry, alleging Cora had gone up North and had a white baby. Price received the stern warning his daughter and new son-in-law had better get me out of town, or there would be trouble. So, in the wee hours of the morning, my folks cut their visit short and slipped quietly out of town. They decided to stay in northern Indiana permanently after that episode.

My earliest memories of Gramps and Mama Lucy, my grandmother, weren't in Doc's beloved Frenchmans Bayou where they had a nice home with a garage, a new car every other year, and a television. Instead, it was their lives in Chicago's rough West Side with its gangs and working-class families. They made their home in a three-story apartment building near a main east/west thoroughfare. Gramps earned a living as a handyman working on West Side tenements.

During summers, my parents sent me and my sister, Linda, to spend time with Gramps and Mama Lucy. My Gramps got up to make coffee around five every morning and shortly thereafter left for work, not to return until dusk. My favorite times with him were summer holidays, because instead of getting up to work, we would get up to start the barbecue pit. The man could cook some ribs, and I would watch intently, trying to learn his tricks. It would take years for me to master grilling the way he did, but I learned to love cooking, thanks in part to my Gramps.

All the neighbors up and down the block knew Price Love and his grandkids. He called me "Carolyn" maybe because he couldn't say Calvin. Gramps wore dentures. From time to time, he pulled them out to rest his jowls. His bare-gummed speech was garbled, and when he ate, we laughed as he shuffled the food around in his mouth before swallowing it. He swallowed and swallowed and licked his chops before saying my name. Doc's baby brother, my uncle Charles, would howl with laughter whenever Gramps called me with garbled, toothless calling.

"Carolyn, I need you to run to the sto'." Charles laughed, while I shuddered with fear because the gang boys didn't play. The Blackstone Rangers and other gangs ruled the neighborhoods with strong-armed force. One couldn't just walk in their territory without permission. Those who dared stroll on a gang-controlled block would face a possible beat-down and the loss of all their money. If you acted scared, the toll would be cash. If you acted too tough, the toll would be flesh. Figuring out how to act in order to stay out of trouble took a lot of thought.

One day, Gramps ordered me to a nearby grocery store for some condiments. Sure enough, I had walked one block from the house when a hard-looking gang boy approached me from the entry of a dilapidated brownstone. He scowled menacingly squarely in front of me.

"What you doing on this block, boy?"

I froze as time stood still. *Now what?* I needed a savior. I noticed a brown-skinned lady wearing a polka-dot bandana watching from the second floor of the brownstone we stood in front of.

She said, "Leave him alone, fool. That's Price Love's grandson."

The gangster boy shrugged and pointed his finger at me. "Watch yo' self, nigga."

After that, I never walked to the store or anywhere else without my uncle Charles. I couldn't have imagined then that many years later, Chicago would present another dangerous foe. Price Love, my beloved Mama Lucy, Uncle Charles, and the lady up in the brownstone would not be there to save me.

My love of cooking paid dividends. When I turned fourteen, Pops helped me get a job as a short-order cook at a rundown burger joint. At that time Pops served as one of the few black policemen with the city of Fort Wayne. The manager gave all the policemen free coffee and hamburgers. I guess that entitled the restaurant to extra police protection, which Pops in turn parlayed into a job for his young son.

Thus I fulfilled Doc's mandate to have a job in my early teens just like my uncles. When the burger joint closed, the owners moved me to another one of their stores, Lucky Steer Steak House, where I continued my training as a short-order cook.

While improving my cooking skills and work ethic, I also learned to spit-shine Pops's boots and shoes to a high gloss so he could see himself in them. I prepared his police uniform everyday by attaching the brass buttons to his standard-issue blue shirt and making sure the navy blue trousers were pressed.

Pops worked two full-time jobs as long as I could remember. He simply wanted to provide my three siblings and me with a better life than he had. He had grown up the son of a dirt-poor sharecropper in rural Arkansas. Price Love had a fit when Pops wanted to marry his baby girl. So, over the years, Pops had a lot to prove. Proving himself meant being able to take care of his four kids and Price's daughter. In the end, Price came to love my father like one of his own sons.

When Pops wasn't working, he kept me in tow no matter where he went. He finally had the son he always wanted. For years Pops and I got haircuts every other week. That meant I got to go on trips to the barber shop. The barbers held court with other men my father's age. I listened closely to the exchanges between the men in the shop. They drank sodas, read *Jet* and *Ebony* magazines and talked about sports, politics, work, and women.

It seemed every man in the shop understood the art of having several female companions. We would drool over the *Jet* centerfold; a voluptuous, beautiful black centerfold model clad in a bikini.

"Man, check this out. She sure is fine! Damn…"

Pops was no exception to the multiple women rule. He loved the ladies, and working as a policeman gave him plenty of access to them. Occasionally, he joined in on the storytelling in the barber shop.

After one such visit, Pops took me for a ride. I couldn't have been more than eight or nine years old. We stopped in front of a strange house, and a woman ran out to the car. They engaged in very friendly conversation. They locked in a face-to-face stare with no personal boundaries between them. Their strong magnetism and hushed tones left me out of the loop for several minutes. She paused when she finally noticed me. Pops never even looked around.

He said, "It's okay. He can see this. It's no problem."

What was I seeing? As we slowly drove away, Pops checked his rearview mirror repeatedly. My curiosity boiled over.

"Hey, Pops, who was that?"

"That's my friend, son, just my friend."

I used to wonder why most of the black men I knew felt comfortable having several women. Was it the mindset and custom borne out of the slavery practice of moving strong black men from plantation to plantation to sire children? Or did something else drive this behavior? I listened closely and learned well. Pops's actions showed me how men interacted with women. I applied some of these things later in my life, some of which lead to heartache and embarrassment.

Doc figured it all out too, because women eventually became bold enough to call the house for Pops. This resulted in many intense late-night shouting matches. The fighting would wake my sisters, brother, and me. The tension settled around the house, thick and unbearable at times. I didn't want Pops to leave, but I always knew he would one day.

After arguments, they would communicate with each other in an interesting way. They did so by playing 45 rpm records on our beautiful 1966 Astro Sonic Magnavox French Provincial console stereo. My dad would play B. B. King's "The Thrill Is Gone" and my mom would counter with Ray Charles's "Hit the Road Jack." This bizarre communication would continue for an hour or more, until one of them left the house. Usually my dad left first. I secretly enjoyed this discourse and couldn't wait to see what song would be played next. After all, we had a large stack of R&B 45s just waiting to deliver a succinct singing message.

A key lesson emerged for me through the debate. I made a promise to never fight with my wife or divorce once I got married. Many years later, I broke this promise and would have to work through that issue during a time when I desperately needed stability.

By 1974, Pops had moved on to other conquests and I found myself as the man of our house. In some respects, it was a situation he had prepared me for from the moment I received my first paycheck. When I proudly displayed my first hard-earned wad of cash, he uttered a sentence that changed me forever.

"Boy, offer yo' mama money first before you do anything with else with it."

"What?"

"Give your mama some money first before you do anything else with it."

I stared at him blankly and my face got red hot. What a shocking concept! He hadn't made me do that when my best friend and I worked our paper route. What was this all about? While my friends were having fun after school, I had to rush across town to get to work immediately after class and cross-country practice. This meant late-night homework sessions for me nearly every school night. I cleaned smelly grease pans, washed a mountain of dishes, and mopped sticky floors late into the evening four or five nights a week. Doc hadn't lifted a finger to deserve any of the money I worked so hard for.

I knew Pops wasn't fooling around. His eyes narrowed and he put his oversized brown hands squarely on his hips. That's all it took. Submission came crashing back as I mentally relived the experiences of him "whupping" my naked behind or jamming the butt of the big black standard-issue Fort Wayne police department nightstick under my armpit. I glumly fanned a row of tens and twenties in front of Doc's face. To my astonishment, she slowly grasped then pulled several bills from my hand.

"Thank you, son."

My heart sank. I retreated to the bedroom I shared with my baby brother and climbed heavily into the bunk bed.

This scene played out repeatedly during my high school years. After Pops left home and I worked more and more hours, those tens and twenties helped with mortgage payments, groceries, and clothes. In his own way, Pops had taught me how to provide for my family even before I graduated from high school. He taught me many other life lessons, but this one had lifelong application.

On a blustery holiday afternoon, Donald P. Eckrich, the chairman of Beatrice Foods and the son of the founder of Eckrich Meats walked into Lucky Steer for lunch. He and his senior team had been coming into the restaurant for months. We all knew they were Eckrich executives and tried to out-do one another, brown-nosing and serving them cup after cup of coffee. Deep in the recesses of my mind, I thought that if I played this thing right, I could end up working at Eckrich Meats and be set for life.

So that Christmas Eve when Mr. Eckrich calmly told me he knew someone looking for someone like me, I nearly shouted right there in the cafeteria line.

Yippee, Eckrich, here I come! Our troubles are over, Doc. Hallelujah, thank you Jesus, Praise God Almighty!

Then the praise party stopped as suddenly as it began.

"Do you have a résumé?"

Uh-oh…what was a résumé? *Answer him, you dummy…don't just stand there, fool, answer him!*

"Uh, sure," I lied.

"Good, let's talk more after the holidays."

I spent the next several days frantically trying to figure out what a résumé was and how I could get it prepared before the next time I talked to Don. In later reflections, I asked myself what separated me from the others who cooked and served coffee refills to these men? Several possibilities came to mind, one being: my parents taught me to look people square in the eye during conversations, so I always made a connection when I talked to anyone. I had a warm smile that said "there's no one else in this room but you, and you are my best friend."

I flashed the smile as often I could. When a warm smile is coupled with the frequent use of a person's name during conversation, the recipient is captivated. On top of that, I talked incessantly and loved a good quip. I never met a stranger and was at ease with virtually everyone I met.

Of course, Doc thought this serendipity had to do solely with divine destiny. She believed I got the chance to change my life simply because I had been faithful in taking care of her, my sisters, and brother after our father moved back to Arkansas with his new wife. I couldn't disagree with that, but she also said that I had a pleasing, soft-spoken voice that disarmed people. I never raised my voice even when calamity engulfed me. I worked hard at being affable with a soft touch, which drew people in. I guess Mr. Eckrich noticed those things too.

A few days later in January 1978, Don shared that he sat on the board of directors of Lincoln Bank and had told the chairman all about me. Furthermore, I should expect a call from the vice president of personnel. Sure enough, just as Don promised, I received a call from the vice president. He scheduled an interview during the last week in January, and my heart filled with anticipation as the day approached.

In 1978, Lincoln Bank and Trust Company enjoyed its rank as the largest bank in the region with assets over three billion dollars. It had been established in the early 1900s as the German American bank and had a long and proud tradition of being a well-run and conservative financial institution.

Its main headquarters building served as a distinctive Fort Wayne landmark. The proud and majestic main office resembled a miniature Empire State Building. For many years, it stood as the tallest building in northern Indiana. Inside, the building exuded opulence. Its exquisite lobby appointments featured ornate reliefs, wrought iron fixtures, and a two-story high ornate ceiling Michelangelo could have painted.

People spoke in hushed tones in the grand lobby, because one's voice would echo in the grandiose chamber, the main floor that housed tellers, customer service staff, and the senior executive offices. Could it be I might work in such a place? There were few, if any, black faces. The handful of times I had been in the building, I felt as though I didn't belong. This prestigious place appeared to be off limits to common black folk.

Moreover, I had never done any business at Lincoln. I banked exclusively with Peoples Bank and Trust where my father banked. He conducted business with Bill Hayden, the first black bank officer in Fort Wayne. Pops told me I should see Mr. Hayden if I ever needed anything. Accordingly, Mr. Hayden gave me my first and then second car loan and helped me establish a checking account. I cashed my biweekly paychecks at his bank branch located a few blocks from the restaurant. In fact, I knew very few blacks who banked with Lincoln. All this made me a little nervous, but I pushed those thoughts out of my head as the day of the interview arrived. After all, I knew these people—or at least had served them coffee.

Someone forgot to send me the memo outlining job interview attire. On the day of the interview, I made my grand entrance, fortified with the confidence that Don Eckrich, president of Beatrice Foods had paved the way for me, The Chosen One. Every gentleman in the building but me wore a conservative banker's uniform. I hardly noticed that everyone who crossed my path in the main lobby wore either a navy blue or gray suit. Tailored white button-down and stiffly starched shirts keenly complemented each suit. Shoes were spit-shined and ties were relatively thin and fashioned in perfect Windsor knots.

As I rode up the elevator, I couldn't help but notice my reflection in the highly polished brass elevator doors. The only thing missing was disco music. I felt Saturday Night Fever and celebrated my funky life. I looked impressive in my black stacked-heel shoes, high-waist black double-knit trousers, and stunning pink short-sleeved shirt fully complemented by the striped four-inch-wide tie. I pulled out an Afro pick to fluff my huge Afro to perfection just as the elevator bell rang and the doors opened to the personnel floor. My gold wire-rimmed glasses helped me peer around carefully.

If the vice president wanted to laugh at my clown suit, he kept it to himself. He gently explained the bank's strategy of expanding its manager training program. I had come highly recommend by Mr. Eckrich, so he talked with me like an old friend and detailed the work hours, the nature of the role, and the management training curriculum. Suddenly I understood what would happen next. I received a formal job offer on the spot at the same annual salary I earned at steak house. Shrewd negotiator that I was, I held out for $100 more in annual salary. The vice president immediately said yes. Someone had been looking for someone like me.

Chapter 2
THE FIRST ONE

The Making of a Spirit-Filled Token Black

AS THE PLANE GENTLY DIPPED BELOW the high-level cirrus clouds and began its final descent toward George Bush International airport in Houston, blue sky and golden rays of sun burst through the window. I instantly loved this welcoming party as my eyes drank in the lush green terrain below. The waters of Lake Houston and Lake Conroe shot solid smiles at me and winked as we flew over. The pilot's voice cracked over the intercom announcing our triumphant arrival.

"Ladies and gentlemen, we are making our final descent into Houston. Winds are out of the southeast at ten miles an hour, there is a visibility of twenty miles, and the temperature is a mild seventy degrees."

"Did he say seventy degrees? Isn't this January?" I said to the guy sitting next to me.

"Sure did."

Kathleen had been persuasive, and I had been intrigued. I figured she'd ordered this weather to drive the deal home. After all, the pay we discussed sounded quite handsome and compelled me to think nonstop about how much more I could handle a break from the status quo of my personal comfort zone in Indiana.

"Cal, you'll love Houston, and this company is a strong company. You'll thrive here. Wait till you see the call center. It's state of the art."

"Okay, okay, but I have to wait until after Y2K before I can make the trip."

My first trip to Houston found me falling fast. I hadn't even touched the ground, but the Indiana glacier seemed ten thousand years away, fleeing from my memory at light speed. The first impressions were pleasing. My life had been a life of firsts, and as the plane continued its slow drift downward, my mind once again danced backward a couple decades to other firsts that came to define my life as a young man.

* * * *

During the mid 1960s, Lyndon B. Johnson built his Great Society promising health care, jobs, civil rights, fair and equal housing. While he was busy with that project, I played ball and grew up on Fort Wayne's near east side.

My contribution to fair housing was helping Doc keep our house clean. I was the eldest of her four kids: a tall, skinny-legged, light-skinned lad with a flattop hair cut and black-framed glasses with Coke-bottle lenses. I couldn't see anything without those glasses. My vision was an abysmal 20/200. Because of my bird legs and four eyes, I got teased mercilessly by school mates and neighborhood kids. I looked like a young, skinny, mulatto Clark Kent. The teasing made me shy and reserved. I made up for this pain by trying to be the smartest kid in school and goody-two-shoes at home. That didn't always work.

The fighting with my sisters never ceased. My chubby sister Linda received the brunt of my teasing. I made fun of her chubby frame every chance I got. I would sneak candy out of Doc's purse and throw the empty wrappers behind the living room couch. I ate sugar out of the sugar bowl, spilling some all over the kitchen in the process, and blamed it on Linda. After she got a "whupping," she would come looking for me when the coast cleared. The fight would be on. I pretended to be Cassius Clay, peppering Linda with stinging jabs to the face. I taunted her as I administered whippings just like Clay taunted Sonny Liston.

"I'm pretty. You're ugly. Float like a butterfly, sting like a bee!"

All the boxing techniques of the world champ didn't do any good once she grabbed me. I would cry, and we both would get it from Doc. Our mom took great pleasure in whipping our behinds for any minor infraction of the household. Sometimes Pops would just laugh and shake his head as she spanked us.

"I ain't raising no bad-ass kids! Now get somewhere, and sit down!" We would run away wailing and humbled.

Doc ruled with an iron hand and doled out more punishment than Pops ever did. I feared Pops more because he had a technique that would reduce us to a level of unsurpassed wailing and terror. His trick was pulling down my trousers and underpants before flailing away with his belt on my bare behind. I never wanted him to follow through on his threat to whip my naked bottom because the spankings he inflicted hurt so badly. Sometimes I faked crying during whippings from Doc to make her abbreviate my punishment. I never had the opportunity to fake anything during my Pops's spanking because the licks took my breath away.

That's exactly what happened to me the day Pops and Doc left me in charge of my sister Carla and baby brother Rod. I loved Rod. I always wanted a little brother. I proudly protected him from the dangers of my evil sisters. Carla irritated me more than Linda ever did. That particular day, she mouthed off to me, pushed Rod down, and made him cry. This totally honked me off. Just as Cassius Clay would have done, I floated like a butterfly and stung her like a bee. After the precision punch, she screamed and grabbed her mouth. I almost had a conniption when I saw blood gushing from her face and noticed I had knocked her two front teeth loose. Gripped by horror and fear, I begged her not to tell. It was no use. She cried for an hour. Her natural "high yellow" face had turned totally beet red by the time my parents came home. I got the whupping of my life that day.

The firstborn child is always the tool for parental learning and practice. The continuous teaching started with my name. It wasn't really Calvin, it was "boy."

"Boy, grown folks is talking, get out of here!"

"Don't answer me 'what,' boy. You better say 'yes ma'am' or 'yes sir' when we talk to you."

"Boy, I'll whup yo' naked ass if you don't straighten your face up now!"

I lived my life doing the beck and call of Doc and tried as hard as I could to avoid whuppings for being disobedient or moving too slowly after a command. She worked me like a servant in the big house. I scrubbed, mopped, and waxed floors, made beds, dusted, cleaned toilets, and washed baseboards. I made sure the living room, with its plastic-covered French Provincial furniture, always looked like a showroom. All this domestic duty contributed to my becoming a total neat freak for the rest of my life. So when I visited other people's homes that were not perfectly clean, I was put off.

Once I visited my cousin's house, and it was a total mess. My uncle hadn't done as well as my father and his house reflected that. Clothes were strewn about the bedrooms. Beds were unmade. The kitchen looked as though it hadn't been cleaned in days.

My cousin and I were busy playing in the front room when out of the corner of my eye I saw something dart across the kitchen floor. I looked again, and saw a gray rat the size of a small cat. I screamed and ran to the front door.

"What's the matter with you, boy?"

"Pops, there is a big ol' rat in the kitchen. Can we go home right now?"

My uncle nearly shouted. "Boy, ain't no rats here." He moved close to my daddy and glared at me.

"Daddy, please, let's go!"

Sure enough when the others looked in the kitchen, the king of vermin stood in all his glory, big, gray, and unafraid. He stared at us with utter contempt and then dismissal. My uncle retrieved a broom and chased him. The rat ducked into a hole near the stove just before the killing blow landed.

Pops just laughed. I ran to the living room couch and sat frozen in terror until we left for home. I kept my eyes trained on the kitchen. When all the fervor died down, that big rat wobbled back to the middle of the kitchen floor and stared at me. After that night, I gladly helped Doc keep our home spic and span. The fear of rats and mice was a motivator to scrub all the more and become a lifelong neat freak.

My best friend and next-door neighbor, Michael, and I were excited about the upcoming school year at McCullough Elementary School four or five blocks away from our homes in Fort Wayne's all-black East Central neighborhood. Unbeknownst to me, the grown-ups had a different plan for us. They had heard about President Lyndon Johnson's Great Society; we hadn't. Just before I started fifth grade in 1966, there were meetings at a local Baptist church. Doc and Pops listened as the fire and brimstone preacher shouted to a sea of black faces.

"Our kids deserve a better education."

The congregation affirmed in a thunderous crescendo.

"Amen!"

"Say it, Reverend!"

"That's right."

The congregation pumped angry fists and shouted. I felt confused. Next thing I knew, instead of making the daily short walk to my school, I traversed several blocks the other direction to attend a Freedom School. The two-story, yellow-brick building was better known to all of us in the neighborhood as the "Y." It felt weird to begin the fifth grade at the Y, because all the kids met there to play basketball, do arts and crafts, and hang out.

Before long, the hoopla started to subside. A couple weeks later Doc cried as she watched me board a big yellow bus in front of McCullough Elementary to take a trip across town to Indian Village Elementary, my new school in an all-white neighborhood.

There were six desegregated fifth-grade students at Indian Village. We stuck together at first. Then slowly, we began to play with the white kids even though they talked funny. Recess at Indian Village elicited pure wonder and delight as the sprawling green lawn provided the perfect place for running and frolicking. I loved to run. My legs carried me faster than every kid at Indian Village. The one square block of cement we played on at McCullough School couldn't compare to this oasis.

One day competition during recess got a little rough. My new friend,

Willy, stopped in his tracks and glared at me after I shoved him hard to prove a point.

"Nigger!"

No white person had ever called me this awful slur to my face. It took three people to pull me off of him. I felt heat all around my head. My heart pounded loudly as I looked down at my grass-stained trousers. I knew I would have to explain this and surely would get a "whupping" that night.

"I hate this place!"

But after I calmed down, I realized that wasn't true at all. I excelled in the classroom and earned good grades. I loved the cafeteria and my teacher. I'd made a ton of new friends. I enjoyed the library most of all, and I couldn't wait for our time there. I had made a promise to myself to read every book in the library. My love affair with reading and books truly began at Indian Village, and so I checked out as many books as allowed each time I visited.

Adapting to new surroundings carried over to 1968 when my parents decided to move to a home on the south side of Fort Wayne. There were few if any other black families in the neighborhood. Interestingly enough, the white flight that normally accompanied such a move began slowly at first. I had heard the stories about how whites moved from integrated areas because the presence of black families drove property values down.

Many believed one of the first casualties of a property acquired by a black family was the lawn. Black people killed grass. I pledged to keep our yard nice, so I volunteered to help Pops keep it mowed and manicured to perfection. One particular day, I had spent virtually hours trimming, pulling weeds, and mowing. Pops had been watching me on and off. He usually kept our yard pristine.

"Boy, why you working so hard on this yard today?"

I didn't know how to tell him I didn't want our yard to look so bad that the white neighbors would snicker. I cared about it as much as he did.

"I'm just trying to help, Pops, that's all. You work all the time."

"Thanks, son."

I continued my newly acquired talents of making friends with white kids and speaking "white" or "proper" English dialect. This skill would serve me well for years and years. Whether some people accept it or not, there truly are cultural and linguistic differences between whites and blacks. I learned early on that, in some cases, whites responded to blacks based on how they spoke. So I worked on toggling back and forth, depending on the situation.

I'm sure that skill specifically helped me as I served coffee at the steak house and navigated through the management training program at Lincoln Bank. I had become fully bilingual. When I was around whites, I spoke proper English, the way I had learned by listening to the kids at Indian Village and up and down my street. When I spent time with family, at church or hanging with black friends in various settings, I could easily and quickly resort to the comfortable sing-song dialect of my people.

The few times I didn't toggle quickly enough caused teasing and catcalls from my black buddies.

"Damn Calvin, you can't be Tommin' around here. You'll get yo' ass kicked."

No one liked an Uncle Tom. I wouldn't dare let on that I had fallen head over heels for a white girl who lived down the street from me. I'd never hear the end of that.

After nearly a year in management training, the powers that be at Lincoln Bank placed me in a permanent role in the consumer lending department as the student loan officer. The bank had a thriving guaranteed student loan program. For two summers, I pumped out hundreds, maybe thousands, of loans. I made low-interest student loans to the children of small business owners, attorneys, doctors, corporate executives, and city fathers. I got to know the Who's Who of Fort Wayne, because I had the cheapest money in town. The word was out. I made contacts that would last for two decades, because I virtually gave away $2,500 a year to each student loan applicant.

The paradox of this was, while I helped all these young people pursue their dreams and find their way to college, I had dropped out of college because I had "made it." I enjoyed a good income, had bought a brand new Chrysler sedan, and had money to give Doc. The Afro had been sheared, and navy blue suits and shiny shoes filled my closet. Life was good, but I learned something embarrassing about myself one day when meeting a student loan customer who had come in to make repayment arrangements.

One of my duties included contacting graduates and college drop-outs to make arrangements for orderly repayment of their loan. One such graduate was a woman named Marilyn. When I received notice Marilyn was no longer enrolled in school, I proceeded to call her and write letters requesting she contact me or come to my office. No luck. I called the relatives listed on her application, but they were no help. After several months of trying to close the case, Marilyn called me out of the blue and scheduled an appointment for the very next afternoon.

I bragged to my secretary. "Dang, I'm good. I got Marilyn to come in!"

"Wow, that's great, Calvin."

The next afternoon, Marilyn came to my office on the spacious second floor as promised. I had a huge mahogany desk chock-full of loan documents. There were no cubicles; just a long row of perfectly lined mahogany desks for each loan officer in a huge rectangular room with eggshell-colored walls.

When I received customers, I sat behind the desk with the customer's chair on the right side. This arrangement made each visit more casual and comfortable. Marilyn took a seat, and we exchanged pleasantries.

"Thanks for coming in, Marilyn. How are you this afternoon?" Marilyn wiggled in her seat and moved from side to side. She covered her nose and mouth and groaned. Her eyes watered. I was puzzled and leaned forward. "Are you alright, my dear?"

She nodded as she picked up her rather large purse and began to rifle through it. After a moment she pulled out a mint and popped it into her mouth. Once I thought she was fine, I continued to share the repayment terms and conditions with her.

"The guidelines of the student loan program mandate that you begin monthly payments six months after you cease half-time enrollment. Are you still taking classes?"

All of a sudden, Marilyn stood up and stepped away from my desk. She fanned her hands wildly in front of her face and backed away from me. She muttered under her breath, but I had deciphered what she said. "Your breath is awful!

She gathered her belongings and backed away from my desk never to return. Marilyn's loan defaulted. I found out I had bad breath. Our receptionist and my friend, Lavelle, confirmed the horrible accusation. When I shared the story about Marilyn, she simply asked, "How often do you brush? Do you brush your tongue when you brush your teeth? That usually helps."

I have bad breath? I couldn't believe this. *Oh, my God. This is Pops's fault.*

During my childhood, getting ready for Sunday school, Pops helped me with my tie. He would form a perfect Windsor knot. I never wanted to wear a funky looking clip-on, so he taught me how to make the knot. I would go to his bedroom right after he woke up. He would stand over me to demonstrate the technique. His putrid morning breath nearly killed me every Sunday. He smoked Salem cigarettes for as long as I could remember. That only made it worse.

I learned to tie my own tie, so I wouldn't have to smell his awful morning breath. I got so good at forming knots. I could do it with my eyes closed. His bad breath motivated me. Now he had passed the dragon breath on to me! *Thanks, Pops.*

Lavelle didn't buy that story. She had attended the same church my family went to and had known Doc and Pops for years. She commented on my Dad's appearance several times. "You're a handsome man, Calvin, but your Daddy is more attractive than you." My mind wandered back to the barbershop stories. Was this another one of Pops's friends? They were everywhere! Her comments had nothing to do with liking Pops. She felt that way because of my breath. Once I allowed my mind to wander, I recalled all the others who had taken steps backwards or had offered mints as I moved in closer to speak.

I had refused so many offers. What a dummy. No wonder I had trouble getting a steady girlfriend. After that day, I tried to keep mints and gum handy. Even then, I was always worried about bad breath. Had this hurt my career?

Apparently halitosis had not completely derailed my career. By 1980, the bank's board of directors appointed me to the role of officer. I hadn't the slightest inkling this appointment was a huge deal. I was stunned when the president's assistant called me down to the main floor because her boss wanted to chat with me. Why would the president of the bank want to talk to me? Was it my bad breath? I'd seen him in passing and heard him speak at some town hall meetings, but I'd never spoken to the man. Now he wanted to see me. I nearly wet my pants on the way to the mahogany office in the corner of the main floor.

As I crossed the threshold, the silence and feeling of power in that grand office enveloped me. The president invited me to sit down in one of the expensive maroon leather side chairs. As I sank into the comfort of the cushion, it was all I could do to hide my trembling knees. He sensed my nervousness.

"Relax, Cal. This is wonderful news. You've been appointed officer of the bank. This is a historic moment. You're the first African American officer of Lincoln Bank. Congratulations."

He came over to shake my hand. My legs felt wobbly as I rose to receive the congratulatory handshake. Thank goodness I had popped a peppermint in my mouth before making my way to this grand office.

He proceeded to give me a history lesson on the bank. Although I had heard the account many times, I listened in awe as he shared his version of the familiar story. It was 1980 and I had become the first African American officer of the bank in its seventy-fifth year of business. I never forgot the gravity of the moment; one of the "firsts" that pleased me for the rest of my professional life.

By the early 1980s, I had moved from the consumer lending division to the commercial lending division within the bank. The real changes were about to begin for me. I had met Gavin.

Those of us trying to move up into management worked as credit analysts and loan administrators in the credit department. Both were roles that meant we were business loan officers in training and glorified gophers for the vice presidents. The mind-numbing work, which required tedious attention, was performed in a maddeningly quiet area a world away from the grand front lobby and the prestigious executive floors. This relegation to the place of desolation drove me crazy because I thrived on interaction and having fun.

Gavin worked for the executive vice president, so he assumed the role of informal top-dog of our group. Our boss was a short, bald, odd-looking nerd who had worked at a competing bank for a number of years. He fit the caricature of a 1950s banker: white and straight-laced. He told endless boring stories about bankers and business customers from long ago.

My friend Gavin had the perfect cure for our boredom. He could imitate the boss to a tee. He would retell one of the boss's stories while we all pretended to sleep and snore, getting within an inch of us to drive home the punch lines. However, the funniest thing Gavin could do is imitate other people's walks. When our boss would leave the area, Gavin would start the show. We'd call out names, and Gavin would imitate their walk. It didn't matter if the name we screamed out belonged to a man or woman. He could swivel his hips and wiggle his behind like a woman or walked hunched over like one of the old bankers.

One day, our boss walked in as we watched Gavin imitate the walk of one of the hot executive secretaries. Gavin never heard him or saw him coming, because his show was in full production. We all saw the boss walk in, but we were nearly on the floor laughing because Gavin had this particular walk down pat. His toes pointed outward and legs moved in quickstep all as he shook his butt. Our boss glared at us while we scurried like rats running for cover. Gavin got called to the boss's desk. I buried my faced and wiped away tears and coughed away the laughter as I hid in my cubicle.

Almost every Friday, Gavin brought cigars for us to smoke in the afternoon before the weekend started. As we puffed, he began long discourses about a myriad of topics. Among his favorites were the Reagan conservative movement and how the white male was starting to be at a disadvantage because of affirmative action, his sexual prowess, and the importance of portraying a certain behavior in the role a banker.

Many Fridays the discussions became heated. They nearly turned into shouting matches, because Gavin made stupid racial inferences or explained why he should be promoted to lending officer before any of us. I thought he was full of crap, but ultimately he did get promoted. The rest of us had to wait our turn.

Waiting patiently paid off as I eventually achieved another first by virtue of being appointed assistant vice president and commercial loan officer. My pride and satisfaction brimmed. I had returned to college, working in earnest toward a degree, majoring in finance and marketing. The role opened up opportunities for me. Given my status of a young aspiring executive at the town's largest bank, there were invitations to serve on several local boards of directors.

There were write-ups in *Frost*, a local black-owned newspaper, about my promotion and accolades for me in the black community. I relished all this but always tried to remember my humble beginnings, my faith, and my family. Staying grounded meant everything to me. I tried my best to deflect all the attention; however, a problem appeared on the horizon.

As the years passed, being the "first" and or only black became more and more intoxicating. It presented a myriad of opportunities. I found myself wanting to be inebriated with being first more and more. Who wouldn't want to be the center of everyone's attention? Being first facilitated pulling back a veil that covered an entirely different culture and lifestyle largely hidden from the people in my family and those I grew up with.

This new lifestyle intrigued me and finally I'd figured out what I wanted to do in life. If I could become a vice president at a well-respected institution by the time I turned thirty years old, I could surely make it in business. I could become a senior vice president at someone's company. Eventually I would run a company. I set my sights on that goal.

"Doing" had taken over and overshadowed "being" myself, whoever that was. I found myself studying how conservative entrepreneurs thought. Becoming an intellectual and transcending race became a real obsession for me. I threw away my Democratic roots and became a Republican, because Republicans believed in supply-side economics, free markets, and enterprise. These were the principles I learned over the years in the financial services industry, and while they were principles not widely shared in the black community, they were becoming ingrained in me.

Gavin had taught me to scoff at affirmative-action policies. After all, if people wanted to get ahead, he reasoned that all they needed to do was read and study. Opportunities would present themselves. I laughed quietly inside at black people who weren't bilingual just like Gavin did. He laughed outwardly at blacks who used slang and colloquialisms and made it a point to make sure I noticed the linguistic deficiencies.

"Be glad you don't sound like that, Calvin. Did you hear that? Let me 'ax' you. The word is *ask*! Pitiful."

Even though I treated co-workers and staff cordially, there was this idea developing in my head. I was better than others. I was chosen. All my training in Gavin's banking school and small business administration led me down the path of looking at employees as widgets; little more than interchangeable resources. It made me somewhat indifferent and unemotional at times, because I learned to think in very objective terms. I wasn't completely a cold-hearted bastard, but it took a lot to get me emotionally involved if I didn't feel like turning on the charm. A form of arrogance and elitism began to settle on me.

All this drove a great conflict within me. I heard a voice inside.

Sellout.

Uncle Tom.

Those words rattled around in the back of my mind. Being first meant learning more and bettering oneself, even transcending race, but in my heart of hearts I knew bettering oneself should never drive one to the point of forgetting or rejecting one's own culture or beginnings. There were fierce personal battles in many aspects of my life. The firsts weren't limited to Cal the professional. They also happened in my personal relationships and spiritual life. I had grown up as a skinny nerd who tried to fit in two different cultures.

All during high school I worked, went to church, and ran track and cross country. I'd never had a steady girlfriend. I never had time for one. More importantly, despite all the things I learned by observing Pops, I felt totally awkward around girls. My friends all had girlfriends and were good at using lines to secure phone numbers and dates. I wasn't. I literally froze when the conversation centered on going on dates or socializing with the opposite sex. By the time I reached twenty, I wondered if I would ever have a steady girlfriend let alone be married with a family.

Music ended up being the entryway to finding my first wife. My love for music started early on in my boyhood listening to my Pops and friends rehearse gospel quartet music at our house almost every Saturday night. His singing mesmerized audiences. He and his buddies performed fantastic gospel sounds. They made appearances at "singings," which were gospel quartet concerts at different black churches all around town.

Since the rehearsals were in our living room, I had a front row seat for all of them. I learned all the lyrics and every note of the gospel quartet songs. I would sing along on every song. A few times I got bold and sang along loudly. My Pops never got upset or scowled. He just laughed and winked at me. After all, I was his boy.

I tried to do everything he did. His singing the lead inspired people to stand, shout, clap, and lift their hands in glorious praises to Jesus. The sisters would get happy and shout, and the men would listen intently and cheer the group on. It seemed like the same people were at all the singings. Everyone knew the songs and all the quartet singers. Pops had a strong following, especially with the fine young sisters. They would rush up to talk to him after the concerts. Doc would watch closely.

Whenever Pops's group was called up to sing, I would try to go up with them. Pops would gently usher me back to my seat, but I wouldn't be deterred. I would stand and sing lead and background parts right there in my seat. I wasn't the best singer, but I was better than Doc. We'd tease her because she couldn't carry a tune. She didn't care at all and did her share of singing in the pews too.

This music touched my spirit and stirred something inside of me. I began to love going to church, especially for the music, and eventually decided to get baptized and "join" the Baptist church my family attended.

Not long after I got baptized, I heard that James Brown and his band were scheduled to appear in concert at the Memorial Coliseum in Fort Wayne. My parents not only listened to gospel music, they also loved R&B. Music filled our house nearly every day. James Brown held the title of Godfather of Soul. I wanted to see him. A battled raged in my mind about whether I could go to the concert.

"Mama, I just got saved. Won't God be mad if I go see James Brown? Is that a sin?"

"No, baby, God would understand. It's what's in your heart that matters."

We went to the concert at the ten-thousand-seat Fort Wayne War Memorial Coliseum and found our places high above the stage. I stood on my tiptoes to get a better view of the stage. It took me a while to get comfortable. When the lights went down and James Brown started to perform, I found myself looking around to make sure God wasn't showing up to send me to hell. He never showed up and I ended up singing and dancing alongside my parents. I danced the night away at my first concert!

Sundays were full of stirring melodies too. Devotional selections opened every service, but mostly I enjoyed the songs from the choirs at the churches we attended. Over time, gospel choir music replaced quartet singing as my favorite genre. Throughout my teenage years and into early adulthood, I sang in the choir in the tenor section at True Love Baptist Church.

My friend Marshall, the pastor's son, directed the choir and he made us rehearse multiple sessions during the week. By this time in my life, I had started to fill out some. I had graduated from high school and attended college. My tall and handsome frame gave me a little more courage about interacting with women. All the tenors in the choir were hooking up with girls in the choir or in the church. I had my share of the action, but I didn't have a steady girlfriend. I enjoyed dating several different people.

I began to notice a very nice young woman with big brown eyes and an Afro in the alto section. She had a cute little son who would sit like a perfect gentleman during rehearsals which lasted two hours sometimes. I could never get up the nerve to say anything to her, and she would always leave the moment rehearsal ended. No one seemed to know anything about her, even Marshall, and he knew everyone. He was interested in girls just like the rest of us.

One autumn evening I called on a female friend from the church. As we relaxed on a big soft couch in the shadows of the living room, we heard a gentle knock at the door. When my friend answered the door, a woman with a perfectly styled Afro, clad in a white jump suit, walked into the shadowy room. It took a moment for my eyes to adjust... It was her!

The young woman from the choir with her son burst into the room turned on the lights and flashed a huge smile.

"Hey, Aunt Bern! What's up?"

Aunt Bern? As my friend introduced us, I covered up the awkwardness I felt with what I hoped was charm.

"This is my aunt, Bernice, and her son, Darrell."

"How you doing?" The alto voice was sultry. "You guys having fun?"

I froze; couldn't speak. *Man, her aunt! There's no way.* This piece of bad news preceded another. The second piece came as she began to talk about "June," the little boy's father. They lived together. She had come by to pick up something from her older sister. I can't even remember what she came to borrow. It didn't matter because I would never get my chance. She was unavailable. She had a man from her hometown in Alabama, and they had moved to Indiana together to raise their son. They weren't married, but she left rehearsal quickly to get home. Why should she stick around and have guys like me try to hit on her? All was lost.

Our pastor hired Vincent, a choir director, to help Marshall develop our choir and put us on the road to recording a gospel album. Vincent did his job well. We learned how to sing in perfect three-part gospel harmony and soon were arguably the best choir in northeastern Indiana. He took me under his wing, and I became his friend and confidant.

Vincent also made his mark with the women in the choir and in the church. Soon he had a reputation of being a real womanizer, and he lived up to it. He had several women. His phone rang constantly. If the women weren't calling, they were stopping by for a visit. Like my Pops, Vincent proudly discussed all the women in front of me. My heart raced and a bead of sweat ran down my forehead the night he asked me if I ever noticed Bernice.

"Man, she is fine, but what does it for me is how she takes care of that kid. That's a good woman. She ain't like these others. I'll bet she knows how to take care of a man." He laughed a wicked laugh. "I want you to do something for me, Calvin. Tell her I want to meet her and take her out."

"Why you want me to do it?"

"Don't worry 'bout that, just tell her."

After the next rehearsal, I ran to the back exit of the church near where Bernice parked her car so I could chat with her and deliver Vincent's message. My plan worked to perfection. When she reached the secluded rear exit, we were all alone.

"Hi."

"Hi, Calvin." She kept walking toward the exit door.

"I have a message for you."

"Oh really? From who?"

"Vincent."

"Yeah, what's that?"

"Well, he wanted me to tell you that he liked you and that he'd like to take you out."

She giggled. "He's been with every woman here."

"But he likes you and wanted me to tell you." I repeated this line because I didn't know what else to say. I felt stupid for being Vincent's errand boy. She saw my trembling hands.

"If he likes me, he should have enough courage to tell me himself."

"Yep. That's right. Let me tell you this. I like you and I'd like to get to know you too."

"What about your friend?"

"He ain't here, so I have to speak for myself."

She touched my face. "Aww, that's sweet. I gotta go. We can talk later."

I had betrayed Vincent, but I didn't care. I had to pursue this woman. Vincent was right. If she took good care of that boy, she could make a good mate. And I knew I could be a good father and husband, because I had taken care of Doc and my siblings. Some of my friends were getting married, and I feared no one would ever marry me. The prospect of eternal loneliness worried me deeply.

Over the next several months we talked often. At first, we had to sneak around, because she still lived with June. Eventually, she left him and we began to date in earnest. We were married within two years after I tried to set her up with Vincent.

We made a great team in the early years of our marriage. We were both active in the church and were serious about our study of the scripture. However, singing in the choir was the thing that kept us busy and tied together. Our life centered on going to church. We were there every time the doors opened. It seemed as though we attended business meetings, Bible studies, prayer meetings, and choir rehearsals. Our pastor demanded that of choir members and his parishioners in general. This took all of our spare time in the evenings and on the weekends when I wasn't working. At times, it took a toll on family life. I began to secretly wonder if God really demanded this of his followers or if this derived from the selfishness of the pastor.

Marshall formed a small group of singers to try to garner a recording deal. My wife and I were both in the group. We traveled and sang all over the country. We went to the recording studio to sing jingles and background tracks for other aspiring singers. When our first baby, Kristi, was born, we packed her up and took her with us to concerts. When our son, Geoffrey, came along, we did the same thing. Our three kids were always with us.

There were several of us in the group, and we pushed each other in our knowledge of scripture. We would hold impromptu Bible studies and hold each other accountable to live according to the scripture. I did not smoke, drink, or use drugs and lived a pious life.

I started to reject the teachings of my beloved pastor of many years, because I didn't think he had enough education to teach me anything more. I thought he concentrated too intently on making the audience "get happy" or "shout" rather than teach scripture as much as he should while he delivered sermons.

The straw that broke the camel's back occurred one Sunday when I sat in the front row of the choir loft directly behind the pulpit. Pastor preached a fire and brimstone message and engaged in a long discourse about a faraway valley mentioned in the Old Testament. Suddenly, he turned around and noticed several of us with Bibles open, reading feverishly, trying to make some sense of it all.

"Close those Bibles while I'm preaching."

My face got hot and my eyes narrowed as I returned his glare with my own. I couldn't handle this personal affront to my intelligence. The members in the pews gasped and whispered. At that moment I wanted to get as far away from that place as I could. Marshall looked bewildered as he watched this exchange from his seat at the organ.

I left that Baptist church never to return as a member. The incident prompted me to take all the religion courses I could in the solemn effort to learn what I really believed in. I began the practice of reading and studying the scriptures even more incessantly than I did when our singing buddies pushed each other to do so. I had a stack of concordances and several text books and writings about religions of the world. I obsessed in reading spiritual writings to understand the underlying mysteries of the scripture and unlock their true meanings, never having to rely on anyone to teach me again.

I had put away the pure emotional underpinnings of my religion and became concerned only with the intellectual components. I began to listen to ministers very carefully to see if what they said matched the things I had learned from the various religion courses I took while at college. I became a spectator and critic when I went to church. Preachers, in particular, received a healthy dose of my personal skepticism. They perpetrated too much form, fashion, and self-serving interest in my view. It all turned me off.

Even though my thoughts about the organized church had started to change, I loved God all the more. Studying the scriptures helped me understand I needed to serve others. Over several years, I taught Sunday school classes, sang in the choir, and served as a deacon and as a worship leader.

Some people suggested that I hid from the call into the preaching ministry. The thoughts of pursuing the ministry were interesting, but I liked business so much more and never really felt the "call" to preach. Besides, I had a healthy dose of skepticism when I heard someone say they had been "called to preach," especially if they hadn't previously pursued any formal training. I had seen too many hypocritical and unschooled preachers.

All these events contributed to some crazy paradoxes in my life. Being "first" had made me arrogant and self-righteous to a fault, but all along, I knew something felt fundamentally wrong about this. I was primed for a hard lesson. Little did I know that one awaited me that would change me the rest of my life!

Chapter 3
WHAT IS A DISCONTINUITY?

Climbing the Corporate Ladder

I HAD SPENT ALMOST FIFTEEN YEARS at Lincoln Bank and had achieved wonderful things. However, clouds of uncertainty hung over the bank's landscape. The climate got chilly as the business fundamentals of the bank began to spiral out of whack. There were excess loan defaults, and the bank regulators were keeping a watchful eye on things. The whispering of failure traveled around the central office and at times the staff huddled to nervously discuss the bank's future.

Like a predator stalking weak prey, a huge regional bank based in Minnesota stood poised to take over Lincoln. This couldn't have boded well for me. My counterparts in commercial lending and I were the guys employing an aggressive lending strategy as opposed to the conservative, tried-and-true, uptight business practices of most banks. A blanket of doom and gloom covered the executive floor and people were bailing. I surmised that I might be in trouble and swept out of a job along with several other executives.

All this took a personal toll on me. I lost sleep as I tossed and turned every night in fits of anxiety and would wake up drenched in sweat. I'd never been part of failure on any level. Besides that, my wife had decided she wanted to stay home after Geoffrey's birth. We had moved into a large house and now had three young children. My confidence about holding on to my job and my future as an executive waned. I thought the timing of quitting her job was bad. I went along with it, but I quietly resented her for adding that pressure to me. Passive-aggressive behavior welled up in me and took over. She and I fought over silly things such as the role of corporate life and whether it mattered where people went to college.

The hottest topic starting most of the fights centered on my family, especially Doc and my siblings. She convinced herself my family didn't like her. All the wariness stemmed from some distant alleged chatter in a hairdresser's shop. Apparently, Doc carried on a discussion with anonymous women in some salon about not liking Bernice before we got married, and the word got out. My wife never let me forget this hearsay even though it was second- or third-hand information. She pouted and scolded me about spending time at Doc's house. This annoyed me and lead to arguments at home because I enjoyed visiting with my mom. After a while a deep rift grew between us. I still loved her, but I liked her less and less. I searched myself and admitted that I wasn't without blame, but I didn't care sometimes.

I thought about the promise I made years before. I secretly wondered if I could keep it. *I'm never getting divorced, and I'll never leave my children.* I agonized over whether I had the strength and patience to break the cycle of broken marriages in my family tree.

During that time I took evening classes at the University of St. Francis. In one business class, I sat in front of Rose, a middle-aged woman pursuing her MBA. She worked in the real estate division at Lincoln National Investment Management Company (LNIMC, which she pronounced *lin-a-mack*), a subsidiary of Lincoln National Corporation (LNC), a huge financial services holding company.

A strange sense of déjà vu washed over me one night after class when Rose shared with me that she knew some people at LNIMC looking for an investment professional in the mortgage loan area. My mind raced back to the words Don Eckrich said to me fifteen years earlier.

"I know someone looking for someone like you."

I immediately knew in my spirit, God was looking out for me. He was in complete control of my destiny. Although very excited, I had an inner peace about all this. Doc didn't. She had read news stories about LNC announcing layoffs and didn't want me to leave the bank which had been so good for me. My sister, Linda, worked at LNC and had a lukewarm response about the idea of me having anything to do with it. I convinced myself they just didn't understand what I would be doing if this all worked out, and I charged ahead.

Although my expertise had been in small business lending, my skills and competencies in finance and business development were transferable and sufficient enough to make the jump to the role of investment analyst in LNIMC's real estate division. The best and brightest talent from all over the country had come to LNC to administer a gargantuan investment portfolio.

I felt right at home in this environment. Surprisingly, a contingent of African American professionals was dispersed throughout LNC. The group networked extensively and had established the Black Officer's Network, which was formally sanctioned and supported by the senior-most executives at LNC. This senior executive support of promoting African American officers differed from what I had grown accustomed to at the staid and ultraconservative bank environment I had recently left. I wasn't the first and only at LNC, but one of many. How refreshing.

What I loved most about my role involved the frequent travel to major cities. The territory my team covered included the entire region of country east of the Mississippi. Our marching orders were to make loans to developers on investment-grade commercial properties in markets with a population of one million or more.

Man, did I rack up the frequent flier miles! I traveled to Boston, Philadelphia, Washington, D.C., Richmond, Charlotte, Columbia, S.C., Atlanta, Orlando, Tampa, Sarasota, Miami, Fort Lauderdale, Montgomery, Nashville, Knoxville, Louisville, Memphis, Cleveland, and Detroit. The sole purpose of each trip centered on looking at commercial properties and learning each market. I considered investments in office buildings, apartments, and strip shopping centers. However malls, hotels, and warehouse facilities were also on my radar. During the trips, I met some of the best mortgage bankers in the industry and worked with very wealthy developers and real estate investors. I learned how to master business travel and how to find my way around in virtually every big city in the East, Southeast, and Midwest.

Not only did I travel to cities I had only read about, the trips served as a getaway from home. I detested yelling and arguing. It seemed we did more and more of that. I missed my kids during these trips, but I found myself happy to get away from my wife. Ironically I felt the need to get away even though all the while we were very active in our church. I felt hypocritical because people thought we were the perfect couple. We weren't. I started acting just like Pops. I found myself looking at other women and wondering what it would be like to have a liaison.

Notwithstanding these thoughts, things were moving along well at work. I had grasped the business and had become a senior investment analyst when I heard I had been one of fourteen people from across LNC selected to work on a major project sponsored by the senior executive team. What a stunning and humbling honor. Being selected to this project would be another stepping-stone that would take me down a path that would eventually lead to a dark destination lying ahead. In the meantime, there was work to do.

For many of us, there were immediate benefits in participating in the project. We developed a systemic understanding of LNC's business units that most other employees had not experienced before. We learned that change is evolutionary and, in fact, takes place quickly. I learned to ask a couple simple questions much more often whenever I read about businesses making a specific move, merger, or acquisition.

"Why? What are they really trying to accomplish?"

I learned "discontinuities" would affect business in the future. Our team was specifically charged with identifying discontinuities that would change the face of the financial services industry.

What an odd word. Because I loved to read all kind of books and writings, I'd seen my share of obscure and little-used words. I had never heard this one or seen it before participating on the project team. Authors C. K. Prahalad and Gary Hamel discussed the concept in their book *Competing for the Future.* Using the word in conversation would elicit blank stares from people. So whenever the topic of the project came up around the office, team members would first have to explain the concept.

"What's a discontinuity, Cal?"

I'd quote what we learned in project meetings. "It's a long and unfamiliar word to most of us. The dictionary defines it, in part, as a lack of continuity or cohesion; a gap." This sounded corny and canned, but it was on point.

That explanation usually followed a longer blank stare or frown.

"Think of it this way: a discontinuity is an intersection of trends that affects your lifestyle. It creates new rules and opportunities for people who adopt new rules or ways of thinking. On the other hand, it's not just a trend, a new technology, or something that just happens."

"Okay, so it's something that could change your life?"

"Yep!"

I had to admit, the strange concept made me think differently about how the future is derived.

After six months of intense research over thousands of pages of books, journals, and magazines our team came up with several discontinuities likely to affect LNC's business in the future. More importantly, because we spent so much time together traveling to off-site meetings, researching trends, and discussing our theories on business, leadership, globalization, knowledge workers, lifestyles, technology, and consumer attitudes, we made strong and lasting relationships. Each of us became well-rounded, systemic thinkers.

It wasn't all work. We spent many evenings in hotel bars smoking, eating, drinking (a lifestyle change for me as I grew more critical of the confines of organized religion), gossiping about executives, and telling lies. There were cliques within the team. My closest buddies were Dawn and Carlos. Dawn, a brilliant lady from the corporate headquarters who smoked nonstop, called me "Callie." Our gifted fellow rabble-rouser, Carlos, worked as an attorney for one of the Lincoln subsidiaries. We were three musketeers together. Our assignment included learning everything we could about customers together with their preferences, actions, and trends.

Dawn could out-drink almost everyone, and once she got going, the party was on. Her antics made us howl with laughter. She resembled Wonder

Woman because she stood at an imposing six feet tall, sported brunette hair, and piercing brown eyes. Her mind worked at lightening-quick speed. None of that mattered after-hours. Because she worked in corporate, she knew stories about some of the senior executives. After a few drinks, stories about people would invariably come out, or she would make some silly, sexual innuendo or comment, then laugh and say "Oh baby!" Carlos and I would shake our heads. He could keep up with her. I couldn't. We would show up at the next day's sessions red-eyed and tired but dedicated to changing the financial services world.

After months of work and preparation we proudly presented our final report to the project steering committee, the chairman, and his senior team. The final presentation consisted of a short story about the day in the life of a woman subjected to each discontinuity our team thought would shape the framework of future life. Several of us contributed to the cute but powerful story.

In the months following the conclusion of our work, we conducted several presentations of our findings to the business units. At each presentation, my assignment entailed reading the futuristic story about "Katy," the central figure.

We chose that name with the administrative assistant assigned to our team in mind. Katy kept us on schedule and brought us down to earth when we got a little full of ourselves. She also made sure we were properly stuffed with food and drinks and made all the arrangements for lodging and travel. She provided wonderful support and assistance to our team, so naming the main character of the story Katy perfectly honored her tireless service and support.

One of the trips Katy arranged for us was a team-building excursion at the Northeast Indiana YMCA camp facility. This exercise reminded me of an Outward Bound escapade in which a team of colleagues goes out to the wilderness and works together to overcome a series of challenges and obstacles. Two days before the trip, Dawn broke her arm. We weren't sure if she could make the trip let alone participate in the exercise.

The team leaders encouraged her to go because we all promised to work harder to make the exercise meaningful and to overcome Dawn's handicap. Finally, the day came for our adventure.

The course demanded physical skill and dexterity to overcome the challenges. I had seen these episodes on television and scoffed at the participants who acted like wimps when attempting the various stunts. Much to my surprise the course was extremely difficult to maneuver. It took all of us pulling together to succeed. The challenges included blindfolded navigation, floating across a stream on a piece of wood three feet wide, tire swings over gullies, tightrope walks, and scaling a huge wall. The underlying goal meant developing trust and building teamwork. The stronger members supported the weaker ones. I was learning key lessons to becoming an executive.

Our futuristic story always got a great reaction as we offered the audience a very plausible glimpse of what the future could look like for a typical citizen faced with life's day-to-day events. Our collective vision and vivid imaginations about the future inspired the story.

Telling the story came easily for me because of my comfort with performing and public speaking. In my younger days, I sang gospel music with a group that traveled all over the country. In addition, I had taught Sunday school and led worship services at a large church.

Over the years, I delivered presentations to loan and investment committees, conducted interviews with people applying for credit, and worked with entrepreneurs, developers, bankers, and served on boards. Public speaking had become second nature to me, and I enjoyed having an audience to connect with. All this fed my perpetually expanding ego.

The work got a ton of exposure throughout the company. Those of us who worked on the first phase of this multiphased project received plenty of accolades and had access to the most senior executives in each business unit. We were corporate stars and wunderkinds! I got more than my fair share of face time because I actually worked on two of the four project teams.

In the months following the conclusion of our part of the project, virtually every one of us eventually received promotions or moved on to different roles. I had honed the skills of speaking and presenting my ideas clearly and confidently. I also became especially comfortable with contrarian points of view and building consensus to reach mutually beneficial outcomes. All this must have caught the eye of Nancy, one of the co-leaders of our team. Her normal role at LNC was a senior operations executive for the Lincoln Life Insurance Company.

Shortly after we all returned to our regular roles in business units across LNC, Nancy called me to discuss a couple of openings on her new leadership team. She had an opening for a second vice president responsible for back office processing of transactions.

"Cal, I know you would do a super job, and I'd love to have you on my team."

It had been well over fifteen years since I had managed people, and this role called for managing twenty managers responsible for functions I didn't really know much about. It would mean transitioning from an individual contributor role in the investment division to managing a unit of 375 people processing a staggering amount of transactions each and every day.

What a radical change. This kind of move was usually unheard of.

Certainly there were people already in Nancy's division who understood the administration of life insurance and annuity business far better than I did. So my mind fluttered with giddiness when I thought about this idea.

Even though I was surprised by the idea of moving to Lincoln Life to head a processing department, at that time, I had sky-high confidence in my abilities. I understood the direction of the company and my mellifluent voice made me a very effective and persuasive speaker. I had no doubts about the things I had learned over the last year coupled with the fact that I learned new information quickly. Besides, moving meant a huge promotion and another stepping-stone in my ultimate goal of running my own company. Discontinuity is a strange word indeed. If one wanted to find a real-life example of the discontinuity principle in the flesh, he or she would have to look no further than me.

Two weeks later, I assumed the role and responsibilities of second vice president at the Lincoln Life Insurance Company.

Chapter 4

TEAM FUDD AND THE HEART
OF THE STALLION

Getting Fit Pays Long Term Dividends

OVER THE YEARS, I'D BEEN IN many airports, thanks to business travel. Houston's George Bush International reminded me of a small city. It dwarfed the size of most other airports I'd visited. An underground train connected four large terminals. Each section buzzed with people scurrying every which way. Maybe I had been wrong about Houston being a two-horse town full of tumbleweed and cowboys.

After grabbing my luggage from the baggage claim carousel, I walked outside into comforting sunshine. A gentle breeze tickled my face and the warmth massaged my senses. *What happened to the ice and snow?* Winter raged in Indiana, and yet there was no Hawk in Houston! No gray mush, no plowed snow pushed neatly back into corners of parking lots, and no wind chill. I peeled off my overcoat and sweater. A gleeful laugh rolled from my belly. From that moment on, I knew living in Indiana had come to an end for me.

During the short cab ride to the hotel, I rolled down the window to enjoy the January warmth. The hotel's sun-drenched lobby bustled with activity. As I checked in, I noticed several men wearing big black cowboy hats and cowboy boots. Cowpokes were everywhere. I saw them in the open dining area, the ballroom, and gathered outside of meeting rooms. I had never seen this many men clad in western-wear in one setting. "What's up with all the cowboys?" I politely asked the front desk clerk.

"They are getting ready for the Houston Rodeo. It's a big annual event here."

My mind wandered to the "shoot 'em up" movies I'd watched with Pops. He loved those action-packed stories. I wondered what he would think about this scene.

"Here are your keys, Mr. King."

My mind quickly snapped back to the business at hand. Tomorrow would be a big day. I had to meet Kathleen's boss, Carl, for breakfast and an interview. According to Kathleen, Carl held an MBA as well as actuarial credentials. He enjoyed a long tenure in the insurance industry. Carl had a reputation of being demanding yet fair. He would undoubtedly have some interesting questions for me.

I needed to find a way to relax and prepare for the interview. My last job interview went well, but I didn't get the position. That had never happened to me. I wanted to make sure it didn't occur again.

In those days, going for a run provided the perfect escape from stress, nervousness, and tension. Running never failed to provide a great mental break from the day-to-day grind of life. I had competed in track and cross-country during high school, so I continued to exercise for many years. I took competitive running very seriously and practiced hard virtually every day. I loved the way being fit made my body feel. Even though I had a slight, angular build, I felt healthy and strong. Although Pops primarily called me "boy," he also called me "Slim." I liked that nickname much better.

During workouts, sweat would pour out of me, and I felt cleansed. It wasn't uncommon for people to see me running through neighborhoods or at a local park, practicing for road races. I'd wave as I ran by. When I saw old friends or acquaintances, they would generally ask a familiar question.

"You still running?"

"Yep. I have to keep running. If I stop, the Wonder Belly will take over."

I would smile and rub my tummy. I had three distinct personalities: Cal the business executive and great guy; Calvin, who would kick ass and take names; and "WB," (aka the Wonder Belly) who constantly looked for treats. WB expanded rapidly whenever I suffered running injuries and couldn't exercise.

The running boom of the late 1970s and 1980s captured me. I competed with a good measure of success in five-kilometer and ten-kilometer road races. I became a weekend warrior. This meant traveling to towns all over northern Indiana on Saturday mornings to test myself against the clock and other runners. I won a number of plaques and trophies for finishing near the top of my age group.

One September Saturday morning, I entered a half marathon race. This would be my first attempt of that distance. I ran near the front of the throng for the first six to eight miles. The race course wound along country roads and through a scenic state park, filled with trees adorned in the beautiful autumn colors. At mile nine in the park, things began to change. My signature long stride started to chop, and my legs began to cramp. This never happened to me before. As I approached the ten-mile mark at a bridge on the way back to the center of town, I stopped running.

I grew more and more perplexed about my body's reaction to this distance. It suddenly occurred to me longer running events required more training, and maybe even a different approach. I wallowed in disappointment, grimacing with each step. Another runner zoomed past me. After he passed, he looked over his shoulder.

"Hey, Calvin, what's wrong, man? Having a bad day? This is different from a 5K, buddy!"

Who was this guy, and why was he talking to me? What a smart ass. I promised that if I ever saw him during another race, the outcome would be much different. It was false bravado. He pulled away from me as I limped along. There wasn't a thing I could do. Before long, he was out of sight. In fact, many runners passed me by. I walked and jogged the last three miles, moving as slowly as a funeral procession. It was a pitiful outing. I drove back home in total humiliation. My first test at a longer distance race resulted in total and utter failure. To add insult to injury, for the first time ever, several women roared ahead of me during the race.

The following week, I skipped lunch to jog at the downtown YMCA. A guy confidently approached me during a break in one of my workouts. It was the smart-ass who blew by me at the half marathon. *Oh man! Get away from me!*

"Hi, I'm Tom Yoder, the guy who passed you at the bridge at the half marathon. Remember?"

"Yeah." *How could I forget? Okay, get the rubbing-in over with and leave me alone. I don't know you.*

"You had a tough day out there. That's not like you. What happened? Went out too fast?"

He smirked and chuckled as he shook my hand, but his comments weren't mean-spirited at all. He seemed friendly enough. I waited to see how far he'd go with teasing before I told him to get away from me.

"There's an art to running these longer races. Stick with me, and I'll teach you how to do it. You can't just go out there and blast away. You have to take your time, and let the race come to you."

The nerve of this guy! He doesn't know me. I ran people like this into the ground every weekend. He'd gotten lucky. I'd had a bad day; nothing more than that. However, as much as I hated to hear it, I knew "Yoder," as a couple guys called him as they passed by, was right. I decided if I ever wanted to run longer distances, including my ultimate goal of a full marathon, I should probably listen to Tom.

Yoder was a sarcastic bastard who also ended up becoming one of my dearest friends. He had a mercurial wit and intellect that intrigued me. Tom not only taught me how to run distance races, later he taught me about business life. Behind the veneer of sarcasm rested a warm and loving heart. Some would take the time to break the veneer, others would not. I did and obtained the reward of a kind friend for life.

Yoder worked as an ambitious and promising young attorney specializing in business bankruptcy law. He had a group of buddies who were very good distance runners as well as young professionals and business men. Terry worked as a commercial insurance salesman. Like Yoder, Gary was an attorney. Jim owned a home improvement company. Tim earned his living as the chief financial officer at a local corporation. He had the added distinction of being a former state champion in the mile run. Rick worked at an area school as principal and Jerry owned a farm. The teasing among the group was merciless with Yoder serving as the ring leader.

We practiced with other people who participated in triathlons, such as Jon and Scott Beasley (the world class Ironman competitors in our group), and Linda and Brian, who introduced us to riding road bikes. On occasions, Kirk, Ward, and Mike joined us on fitness jaunts. While I trained with this group from time to time, Brian and Scott became two of my closest friends.

Scott helped me select my very first road bike, a black Cannondale, which I nicknamed Black Beauty. Brian kept me laughing all the time with quick wit and teasing. He and Scott rode their bikes like the wind. Keeping up with them as we traversed the northern Indiana terrain was challenging. It never worked. They "dropped" me on virtually every ride. Despite getting left behind, eventually I learned to enjoy a forty- or fifty-mile bike ride in the country on Sunday mornings before church.

One cold winter day, Tim embarked upon on a solo weekend run. One of our team members driving in Tim's neighborhood spotted him on the side of road in full stride. As Tim ran, he wore a plaid red and black hat with flaps covering his ears. This hat resembled the hat Elmer Fudd wears as he endlessly pursues and shoots in the direction of the lovable Bugs Bunny. Tim looked totally hilarious all bundled up in running gear and sporting a smart plaid hunting cap. The description of Tim wearing the Elmer Fudd hat got back to Yoder.

Yoder teased Tim uncontrollably. He couldn't believe a guy serving as the CFO of a major corporation would wear a hapless and inept cartoon character's hat. He decided on a name for our team to honor Tim's now infamous head cover. From that time on, we would be known as Team Fudd or Fudd for short. He would refer to the group that competed in triathlons as the Tri-Fudds. The names stuck. Yoder selected nicknames for each one of us. We used the names to address one another. He chose "The Stallion" as my nickname because of my long, perfect stride and galloping style.

Every year Yoder distributed his *Yoder Rules of Life* list to Fudd. His first funny rule simply said: "If you want to fuck with eagles, you better know how to fly."

Once I got past the profanity, the rule really made a lot of sense, especially when dealing with the rigors of corporate life. Most times, I worked alone, separated from my white counterparts by cultural differences. The list expanded every year and contained some bizarre but relevant topics. We discussed the rules of life during training. Yoder also kept a careful journal of every run. He measured every route we ran down to the tenth of a mile. Workouts meant serious business. We knew the exact mileage and pace planned for each practice run. Yoder would run fifty thousand miles over the next three decades and carefully enter details of each practice into his journal. I was along for several thousand of those miles.

For the next thirty years these people became my close circle of friends. Most days we met at lunch hour for runs. We made our way outside regardless of rain, sunshine, or cold. We were like mailmen. One could count on us practicing outside every day in preparation for the next race. The pace always started easy, as we teased each other incessantly, told lies, and discussed every topic under the sun. The skill level among us was about the same, so we pushed each other as we trained for weekend races. The locker-room chatter after the runs and the treks to Wendy's for salads and breadsticks became a ritual. The Wonder Belly would not hear of eating salad, so usually I enjoyed a juicy cheeseburger.

We served on boards together, took trips together, and celebrated holidays together. We grew older together. We were a team.

Running and biking paid dividends for me in so many ways. I made friends, traveled to race events, and rode in bike tours. I found a safe place of escape from the demons and pressures of my life. My fitness regimen kept me healthy and strong. My mother, father, and siblings suffered from diabetes. My grandparents did as well. I never got diabetes, experienced chronic ailments, or missed work due to illness. I always received a clean bill of health during annual doctor visits. I could thank my rigorous exercise program for these positive results. My heart remained in particularly good shape. My resting heart rate was very low, and I did extremely well during stress tests. At just over six feet tall and 180 pounds, my mirror image reflected a picture of health and fitness. I had become the strong-hearted Stallion, and later I would need every ounce of the determination which helped me become a perfect specimen.

Chapter 5
FRIENDS AND COLLEAGUES IN HIGH PLACES

The Good, Bad, and Ugly of Being an Executive

MY FIRST MORNING RUN IN HOUSTON went fabulously well but not because of the special scenery. The route wasn't scenic. While the hotel had comfortable rooms and nice décor, it was located in North Houston near Greenspoint Mall. The locals called it "Gunspoint Mall," because robberies and all kinds of malfeasance in and around the mall were common. Even though several large companies called the Greenspoint area home, the surrounding neighborhood had a notorious reputation due to its alleged gang and drug activity. The area boasted class "A" office buildings and several hotels. However, these nice properties were surrounded by several enormous apartment complexes with histories of crimes, drugs, and ghetto life. So, when I decided to go for a quick predawn run before meeting Carl for breakfast, I did so with a tinge of nervousness. Nevertheless, I had a ritual of running in every new city I visited. I wasn't about to break the string. Besides, I needed to relax before the interview.

After the run, I showered, dressed in my best gray pin-striped suit and put on my shiny black Bostonians. I made my way to the lobby to meet Carl, the senior executive vice president of the Houston based company.

As usual, Kathleen had been correct. Carl stood out, and I spotted him easily. We were the only two men in the lobby that morning dressed in neatly pressed gray pin-striped suits. When he started talking about the phenomenon of Fed Ex taking over the package delivery industry, we immediately connected.

"Big Brown has all those trucks and a long history of customer service. Why is it that that Fed Ex has been able to come in and dominate market share?"

I couldn't believe my ears. What a softball question. I jumped right in.

"Discontinuity."

"What?

39

"Discontinuity." I repeated the weird term with more confidence, capturing Carl's attention.

"Fed Ex changed the face of the industry by promising overnight delivery anywhere. It employs a state of the art hub and distribution system and therefore can deliver parcel faster and cheaper." I had seen the Fed Ex hub during a real estate due-diligence visit to Memphis. "They can run circles around Big Brown."

Had Kathleen joined us, she would have been pleased with that answer. We seemed to be on the same wavelength from the day we met several years before.

I had assumed the role of second vice president in Lincoln Life's operations division. After Nancy and I exchanged pleasantries, she gave me an overview of her vast division. She picked up the phone.

"I'm calling Kathleen Adamson. She will get you settled into your office and show you around."

"Hey Kathleen, Calvin King is here. Can you come over to meet him? Take him to his office and maybe show him around a bit."

Within a few moments Kathleen appeared at the door, and Nancy introduced us.

The tall, attractive woman with warm blue eyes, long blonde hair meticulously coiffed and draped at her shoulders extended a very firm handshake. Her smile filled the room.

"You go by Cal?"

"Yes, call me Cal." A thought crossed my mind. *My family and group of black friends called me Calvin. My wife called me Calvin.* But at work and other venues I wanted to be known as Cal.

Kathleen had strong working relationships with her counterparts throughout the organization. She introduced me to so many people that day, I couldn't keep them straight. As we walked the building and met staff, Kathleen discussed the various functions of each team. She was a systemic thinker and had her finger on the pulse of the organization. I felt convinced that she could just as easily head the division as Nancy.

The body language of the people she greeted told me employees respected and liked this woman. Kathleen had an easygoing but professional presence that played well with people. I liked her style. This proved to be a good thing. I would be working with her for a very long time. She would support me through an unspeakable personal tragedy neither one of us knew loomed in my future.

"Cal, our division supports life insurance, individual annuity, and employer-sponsored retirement plans."

I nodded. Obviously I had a lot to learn, and I planned on grasping as much I could as quickly as possible. My mind raced. *What is an annuity? Retirement accounts? Think fast, you dummy. You should know about this stuff!*

I remembered these subjects from business school, but my mind went blank in the clutches of nervousness. The moment almost overwhelmed me. I felt awestruck even though I had learned a great deal about Lincoln Life from members on the discontinuity project. I simply had to calm down and remember their description of the company.

Luther, the youth pastor at my church, had a saying that used to make me laugh. I thought of it during those moments. "Fake it, till you make it." He always followed that statement with a huge grin.

Let the faking begin. I smiled. Kathleen continued.

"Lincoln Life is in the final stages of completing a comprehensive business process transformation. We've been working on the project for several months. The company has spent millions of dollars on administrative computer systems, hardware and software."

It all came rushing back. Nancy and the other senior executives had employed a strategy of consolidating life and annuity business administration. The transformation team neared completion of its work just as I joined the organization.

"You're joining us at the right time, Cal. We need your creative thinking and leadership skills."

I'd be doing some major faking for a while, that's for sure.

Kathleen showed me to my new office. The space was a converted conference room overlooking downtown Fort Wayne. Wow, what a view, with a direct line of sight to a gentleman's club down the block! During the years I worked in that office, I never saw anyone go into that club, even during the many times I worked late into the evening. I often wondered how they made any money.

For a brief few moments, I stood alone in the middle of the huge corner office, lost in my thoughts. *How did I get to this place?* I honestly didn't know what to do next. After staring out the window for a while, looking through the desk and credenza drawers and inspecting the office thoroughly, I remembered a saying. "A great leader always surrounds himself with people smarter than he is." That would be an easy thing to accomplish here, because I knew only enough about the department I'd just inherited to be dangerous.

So, I decided to walk around to meet people. I started with some of the managers who were there that first day. In the next few days, I would meet more managers. After I chatted with each of them, I made my way through the department meeting employees. This stroll consumed the bulk of my first day, because I had staff on three floors and two buildings. Even so, the decision to walk around to greet employees worked well. I enjoyed hearing myself talk, but I also wanted to learn as much as I could from listening to the staff.

The managers reporting to me were longtime employees and taught me what I needed to know about day-to-day activities. I spent countless hours with Therese, the smart and energetic manager of one of the processing teams. She realized I had a learning curve, so she worked very closely with me and refused to let me fail. Her teams processed literally millions of transactions annually with very few errors and within the established processing times. Her loyalty and eagerness to work together astounded me. The company had decided to outsource the work Therese's employees performed just before I started working with her. She remained positive through the entire process. I never forgot her patience, devotion, and support during that tough transition. I took careful note of her approach and tried to adopt the same kind of demeanor as I managed people.

I decided in order to augment what I learned from my team, I would "manage by walking around" as often as I could. I adopted this management style, because I believed it would serve me well in the role of operations executive. It stood to reason; the people actually doing the work had a fundamental understanding of what stakeholders of a business want. In addition, since employees use the tools developed for service delivery, they generally had some great insights about how to improve processes. I learned if I used common sense and took a practical approach to problems, things would work out fine. Just as I believed, over the next few months, I settled in pretty well.

Learning the tactical elements came easily, but the business of working with the rest of Nancy's leadership team to develop strategy and direct business presented problems. There were inherent obstacles that made working together challenging. The other members of the team were primarily concerned with their own operations. So was I. We had well-developed business silos and worked on keeping them stocked and productive.

Kathleen didn't fit this paradigm. She always had time for my naïve questions. Because she had been in the organization several years, she knew the key players and had unique insights on how to get things done. She always thought about business problems in terms of the entire operation. I enjoyed visiting her office. Kathleen always helped me connect the dots. I felt a kindred spirit with her. When she transferred to Portland, Maine, to manage an operation, I celebrated with her but had a sinking feeling in my belly. She would no longer be there to confer with me and give me her take on the latest developments within our organization.

Ron, the team member responsible for the call center operation, was a mover and shaker. He played a major role in the transformation project and ruled his team with an iron hand. He had been around Lincoln for a long time. He had both information technology background and business acumen. He could speak the cryptic IT language and translate it for those of us running the business units. The problem with this was Ron thought an awful lot of his talents and ability. He stood short in stature but had a huge amount of self-confidence. He quickly pointed out the faults of others with a stinging tongue. We had a love-hate relationship with him.

My processing teams were often the object of his ire. Whenever we made a processing error, customers would call the call center to complain. He would make wisecracks during Nancy's staff meetings about my processing teams screwing up.

"I can't believe Financial totally screwed up again. They are driving business away. We need to fix these problems and work on some quality control measures. Maybe someone in that area should talk to the agents. I'm getting sick of facing the music."

My blood would start to boil. I gave him steely glares. I wanted to discuss why our call center hold times sucked. I contemplated slapping him, but that silliness had no place in my life then. Besides, this wasn't recess at Indian Village, so I couldn't beat him up and walk away with the ball. I had become a big boy, and I understood sometimes in leadership, being attacked verbally came with the territory. So, I bit my tongue and worked hard to keep the peace.

Ron had bigger issues. He didn't like the boss and felt she was not right for the role she occupied. In his mind, her perceived incompetence hurt our division. Unfortunately, most of us knew he felt those sentiments. Ron's verbal interactions with Nancy were curt and downright insubordinate in my opinion. I wasn't surprised at all when one day she had quite enough. In one fell swoop, our call center executive leader was gone. Nancy called me into her office.

"Cal, I want you to consider running the call center."

I didn't know anything about running a call center. I spewed a complete lie. "Nancy, you know I'm a team player, and I'll do whatever you want me to."

I imagined taking over the call center and watching the entire operation collapse around me. Visions of angry customers yelling at me danced in my head. I didn't want to go anywhere near that role! Kathleen encouraged me. She thought I could pull it off.

I sought the counsel of my longtime friend and fellow teammate, Kenneth. Kenneth and I went all the way back to middle school. I remember getting rides home with him after track and cross-country practice when we were kids in high school. He was a stud. He played sports all through middle school and high school, as did his brothers. They were well-known for their athletic prowess and competitiveness. A track state championship in high school paved the way for a full ride to Purdue University for Kenneth.

He enjoyed corporate business success in his own right, and like me, he joined Lincoln Life after working in LNIMC. Kenneth's path to success ran through information technology, so he struggled some with business concepts. I helped him with business matters. He helped me with technology. We had our share of long evening sessions in my office using a whiteboard to help explain concepts to each other.

"Dog, how do you know all this stuff?" he would ask me.

I'd just shrug my shoulders and grin sheepishly. Having Kenneth on the leadership team felt like having my little brother working with me, but there was nothing little about him. He stood well over six feet tall and sported a solid mass of muscle.

I called him over to my office as soon as I left Nancy. It wasn't time to be proper. I needed to know what my boy thought.

"Dude, did you hear about Ron? Can you believe it?"

"Dog, you knew that was coming, right? He went too far. Nancy shoulda been gotten rid of his ass. I'm glad he's gone. I couldn't stand his punk ass anyway."

Ron wasn't on Kenneth's Christmas card list.

"Man, she asked me to run the call center! I don't know anything about the freaking call center."

"You can do that, Cal. Nobody knows this stuff the way you do. That center needs you. You can fix it and have it hummin'. You da' man, dog! That's all you. You know this stuff!"

Kenneth's comments resonated with me. Others also voiced positive and encouraging words about my suitability for the role. The skeptic in me wondered if my counterparts were encouraging me because no one else wanted the job!

For the most part, customer service representatives (CSRs) have a thankless job. Attrition is generally a real problem to overcome. CSRs burn out if the call volume and staffing level is not in equilibrium. Most of the time, people in those roles don't see any real advancement opportunities and don't feel valued by the management team. I coined a description of the ideal personality type best-suited for the role: "expressive analytical." They have to know a ton of information, synthesize it quickly, and then express empathy and enthusiasm to callers to complete service requests.

That task can be difficult, because some callers are downright nasty. It's as though some people lose their minds immediately after they dial a toll-free number. One never knows with certainty what the next call will bring. There are weird people with foibles or idiosyncrasies in our country. Invariably, those people find their way to a call center queue and subject some poor, unsuspecting CSR to their weirdness.

Sometimes, callers get so angry about service that they demand to speak to the president or chairman of the company. No call center management team really lets that happen. So who gets those calls? The escalation specialists, managers, or the executives who own the service center function. These unlucky souls ultimately have to calm some angry callers. I didn't want any part of that job. It occurred to me Ron had been right about the need for excellence in processing. Even so, I accepted the job.

The act became the watershed event that propelled me into managing and directing call centers for years to come. It was the final piece of the puzzle that would lead me to a life-changing event down the road. The next year, during National Customer Service Week, Nancy wrote a personal note to me that made me glad I'd taken the risk to try a new career path.

Cal,

Wow, what a success story you are! It has been such a pleasure to see you grow into one of our most successful customer service directors. You should be so proud of your achievements and the quality service organization you've put in place. I will never be sorry I recruited you to annuities!! In this week of National Customer Service appreciation, it is a pleasure to tell you how much I appreciate your focus on excellence in customer service.

Sincerely,
Nancy

Shortly afterwards, I heard Kathleen had flown in from Maine. When I stopped by to say hello, she flashed her wide, warm smile.

"Hey, Cal, how's it going?"

"Things are going really well. We are meeting service levels in the call center, and the processing teams are doing okay. I'm learning more and more about our business. How are things in Portland?"

"Good. The business is going well. David and Andrea are growing so fast, and they love Maine. It's so beautiful there."

She fidgeted some and had a hesitant look on her face. I'd never really seen her nervous or uncomfortable. Was something wrong? Then it hit me. She's the boss now!

She chimed in right on cue. "You know Nancy is now running the individual annuity operation, Cal. Steve (the executive vice president) asked me to take on the role of running the employer-sponsored business." She'd been promoted to vice president, with responsibility for retirement accounts for people who worked in schools, hospitals, and colleges.

"You, uh, you'll be reporting to me. I hope you'll be okay with that?" She had a sheepish look on her face.

Are you kidding me? It was the best news I had heard in a while. I was ecstatic. I couldn't think of a better person for the job. I liked Kathleen's style. Over the years, she and I always seemed to be on the same wavelength. Secretly, many people thought Nancy wasn't right for the job running the entire operation anymore.

The facts were the entire operation had gotten huge. This strategic move made sense no matter how one looked at it. There were people in some quarters of the organization that expressed glee over Nancy's reassignment. I thought people with this attitude were ignorant and disrespectful. They should have been ashamed of themselves. Corporate life is tough. I'd learned well that you'd better have thick skin if you want reach the top. Yoder's rule of life about flying with eagles couldn't have been more on point.

"That's absolutely great news, Kathleen. Congratulations! It would be an honor to work with you."

The next few months passed in the blink of an eye. Kathleen had made some strategic decisions which made sense and worked beautifully. She promoted one of Kenneth's lieutenants and gave her responsibility for the processing areas. This move freed me up to concentrate on call center administration. I welcomed the strategy. It was well received by all of us involved.

The new millennium quickly approached. Everyone started to worry about Y2K readiness. Lincoln undertook a wide-reaching computer remediation project, just as many other companies all over the globe did. During late summer 1999, businesses worldwide were well into their respective Y2K initiatives.

One August afternoon, Kathleen called me over to her office. I thought this would be another routine meeting about a call center or customer service matter. This time as I walked in, the pleasantries were very short. Kathleen got right down to the matter at hand.

"Sit down, Cal, I have something to share with you."

I'd conducted enough town hall meetings to know when I'm hearing talking points that set up big news. So I barely heard the background information leading up to the operative statement "…So I've decided to leave Lincoln to accept the role of executive vice president at a Houston based company in Houston, Texas."

It felt like someone kicked me. Not only had Kathleen been the best boss I ever had, I considered her a close friend and confidant. People come and go all the time in corporate life, but this felt different. I found myself fighting back tears even as I congratulated her on the move and promotion. She had worked so hard over the years and deserved this opportunity. An eagle can't fly if its talons are buried in cement blocks.

So just like that, she left, and things were never quite the same. My friend Jim and one of his top young business analysts fresh out of college, Laura, also left Lincoln to pursue opportunities at the Houston based company. The operations team went for weeks not knowing who would succeed Kathleen. The weeks turned into almost four months.

I lobbied hard for the vacant role, as did one of my colleagues, Connie. We both felt we were ready to lead the division. Connie had managed the group relationship management teams, while I directed the processing areas and call center. Both roles should have prepared one of us to take the next step. My competitive nature wouldn't let me think of losing this job. It belonged to me. Years of preparation had positioned me right where I needed to be to continue my quest to get to the very top.

I genuinely liked Connie, but I felt I was more qualified for the vice president role. We met a couple times and promised our loyalty to each other, regardless of which one of us got the job. Even as I pledged allegiance to her, in my heart I thought otherwise. There was no way I wouldn't get the job.

We each had interviews with Steve, Nancy, and another senior executive. Once the interviews concluded, the waiting started. It lasted for over a month. The wait would have been maddening except something happened that made it more bearable for me. Although I didn't know it then, it was the "X" factor that would change my life forever.

An October evening while Connie and I were waiting, my cell phone rang. Kathleen's voice on the other end of the phone made my heart race in anticipation and fear.

"Hey, Cal, what's up?"

"Kathleen! It's great to hear your voice. How are things in Texas?"

"Actually, they are going really well. David is in his new school, and Kent is busy around the house and looking after his mom. All in all, we're settling in."

"That's fantastic."

"How are things at Lincoln?"

"Well, we are working on Y2K. I think we'll be fine now. It's just a matter of getting through it. Other than that, I've been going through interviews and handling business in the call center. Really, nothing special at all."

"Uh-huh, that sounds good."

"Just hanging in there, you know. How do you like American General?"

"Cal, it's wonderful. I have a great boss who is very sharp and has been in the industry a long time. He's demanding, yet fair. The company is going in the right direction. There's a lot of opportunity. In fact, that's the reason for my call."

"Really?"

"Yes! One of the people who reports to me is leaving the company. She is responsible for the area that processes premiums, handles group remittances, and works suspense. You know, just like payment processing at Lincoln."

"Got it."

"I have someone in mind for that role and if that works out, I'll have an opening to fill at my call center. Cal, it would be an executive position. You would be perfect for it. You did a great job with the call center at Lincoln, and this would be a great fit for you."

There were follow-up conversations. Each discussion grew more compelling and persuasive. Even though I kept telling myself I'd never leave Indiana, something inside spoke to me. *Make the trip. Even if nothing comes of it, the experience will be worthwhile.*

The last call happened as I headed home in a driving snowstorm on a cold December evening. It was my sister Linda's birthday. I'd forgotten to send her a card and was making a quick stop at the neighborhood drugstore to pick up one.

"Cal, I'm running out of time. I really can't wait too much longer. I have to make a move soon. I really need you down here!"

After I heard the very flattering salary offer, along with the title of full vice president, I finally said yes. "Okay, okay, I'll fly down. I have to wait until after Y2K though."

The timing was uncanny. Connie and I had checked with each other every day to determine if any news filtered out about as to whether we'd been selected to head the division. In the meantime, I'd been having these serious discussions with Kathleen about joining her team in Houston. Ultimately, neither Connie nor I got the job at Lincoln.

I felt as though a ton of concrete had fallen on me. Then confusion gripped me until I felt totally pissed. I had never interviewed for a job and been unsuccessful. My roll of success stretched all the way back to the days when Don Eckrich referred me to Lincoln Bank twenty-plus years ago. The criticism I received about my interview left me dissatisfied. Nothing I heard seemed constructive enough for me to build on. Connie didn't receive any meaningful feedback either. This scenario left us in total distress, especially since Connie and I reported directly to Steve after Kathleen's departure and during the interview process. Steve had shared with me that he thought I was very talented, and I felt certain our working relationship clicked.

"Just need more seasoning." That wasn't constructive enough feedback for my taste.

Was I a food entree? Being angry can warp the principles you believe are true and right. Was pepper the wrong seasoning? I never played the race card when I had setbacks at work. I started to wonder if all this talk about being the "chosen one" was just a bunch of bull crap. Had Willy from Indian Village whispered into the ears of the decision makers? Like the biblical story of Esther, I had prepared myself "for such a time as this." Something had gone terribly wrong, and I couldn't quite put my finger on it.

My whole attitude about working at Lincoln changed. For a month, I hid the anger in my heart, said all the right things, and looked interested in meetings. On the inside, I seethed. In the end, a hard-working, blue-eyed, blonde vice president from the IT area got the job. Many people in operations were perplexed. Some of them whispered to me about the selection.

"Why would they pick an IT guy with no operations experience to run our division?"

I tried to put a positive spin on the decision. But it simply made no sense. "He's a smart guy. He'll do well. We have to get behind him and make it work, like you guys did for me, when I first got here."

I knew enough about talent selection and corporate politics to know there was more than meets the eye with this selection. After all, just a few years before, Nancy had brought me over to Lincoln Life to run a huge processing area when I had no previous experience doing so. Back then, the rumors persisted she was ordered to bring Kenneth and me over, to achieve some diversity on her team. I tried to dismiss that theory because I had talent and smarts. After all, wasn't I the man who had the right skills to do any job? Surprisingly, even I questioned the offer in the private moments of self-candor.

My new boss reached out to me to say he looked forward to working with me. I responded cordially, but I wasn't happy about the prospect of teaching this guy the ins and outs of operations. I was pissed.

Connie and I commiserated in the days following the announcement. There wasn't a darn thing we could do but move on. People would be watching to see how we dealt with the selection. Acting a fool now might come back to haunt me if future opportunities ever presented themselves. I had said to people I mentored, "Corporate life is tough. You'd better have thick skin if you want to be near the top."

I couldn't understand or control my confusion. On one hand, I felt more than disappointed about not getting the job I really, really wanted. My anger burned so hot until I could hardly function. On the other hand, it felt great to feel wanted and valued by Kathleen. However, pursuing the move she dangled in front of me would mean my life would turn upside down. I had trouble finding comfort in moving. My kids were nearing high school graduation. I loved my church, and my connections in the community were extremely solid. I wasn't sure I had enough courage to make the changes. So, I decided I would just go through the motions of interviewing for the job at the Houston company.

The time had come to swallow some of my own medicine. It didn't taste good at all, but I soon realized that maybe it just wasn't my time.

"Just need more seasoning."

I had a great team and a call center to concentrate on. I began to prepare for Y2K. The new millennium would hold great things for me at Lincoln Life. Even though my quest to continue a steady climb up the corporate ladder hung in the balance, I had little doubt good things still could unfold for me professionally.

Chapter 6
WHEN ONE DOOR CLOSES

Moving to Houston and Making Things Work

THE INTERVIEW WITH CARL WENT DELIGHTFULLY. When we finished our breakfast discussion, he drove me to the call center for a tour and to meet a couple folks. Our drive lasted just four or five short blocks to the other side of "Gunspoint." Strike one.

Strikes two and three never came. As we drove near the entrance of the parking lot, my LNIMC commercial real estate skills kicked in. The call center resided in a two-story, stand-alone office building with a white stone façade and smoked black glass. The building nestled in a cul-de-sac near a busy intersection. George Bush International airport sprawled only five minutes away. The surrounding buildings were all investment-grade office buildings complemented by an upscale hotel. Someone had given careful thought to this location. Although I couldn't quickly count parking spaces, I estimated there were more than enough to accommodate a couple hundred employees.

Lush landscaping, accented by color and manicured to perfection, skirted the campus. The multicolored brick sidewalk led to double smoked-glass doors with a card-key entrance. The double doors opened to an airy lobby, drenched by sun pouring through a tall atrium and ceiling featuring sky lights. On the opposite end of the lobby, two more smoked-glass doors led to a tropical, airy courtyard full of palms, greenery, and cobblestone paths. Teakwood garden furniture and fountains accented the walkways. This space offered the perfect respite to reflect and recharge during busy business days.

Carl introduced me to a couple directors at the call center and then said his goodbyes. Those two directors had been the architects and project leaders for this new call center. Their pride brimmed over as we walked the floor. The call center configuration boasted groups of serpentine clustered workstations equipped with the most up-to-date ergonomics. The interior of the building featured an envelope of white noise, which provided an unbelievable soft

51

backdrop for a hundred simultaneous phone conversations. Contemporary designs, including curved walls and pastel colors, accented the common areas. The work stations were state-of-the-art and provided the CSRs the ability to adjust the height of desks with the push of a button. This layout put my call center to shame. I marveled at this place!

All of the conference rooms in the building were named after a tropical paradise. We entered the Maui conference room. I pulled off my suit coat and opened a diet Coke. I calmed myself and decided just to have fun with this interview. What did I have to lose? I told myself *"Relax, Cal, and do your thing. Just talk. You are 'The One.'"*

We talked for two hours. Their knowledge of call center operations and complete understanding of the employer-sponsored business blew me away. I found myself at a room-sized whiteboard drawing organization charts of my Lincoln organization and call routing architecture. We laughed and talked about projects we would work on together. I couldn't wait to work with them. I shared that sentiment with Kathleen when she picked me up to drive us to her suburban home. We enjoyed a time of relaxation and reconnecting before I flew back to Indiana.

Another round of interviews with vice presidents and directors from all over the company followed a couple weeks later. One interview in particular I would always remember took place with a director in human resources, Tina. We hit it off immediately. Tina also hailed from Indiana but had lived in Texas a few years. Her sharp but pleasant questioning got right to the heart of call center management's concerns.

"What, in your opinion, is the biggest challenge for call center executives?"

I didn't pause at all. "It's turnover. It's so hard to recruit and retain talent, because call center work is so challenging. CSRs get burned out easily, so it takes motivation, creating opportunity, and proper staffing to make sure that doesn't happen."

Tina nodded in approval. I thought she would make a fantastic business partner. It pleased and excited me to see an African American woman in that critical role. Later, we would have a conversation that would help me solve a major personal problem.

Discontinuity had been hard at work. A confluence of events changed the face of my future. Getting snubbed for the job that was rightfully mine, the shiny new state-of-the-art call center, and the series of life events, dating back to meeting Don Eckrich, all did their job perfectly. I submitted my resignation at Lincoln Life the next week.

My ego led me to think my departure sent shock waves through Lincoln operations. It did, but I didn't care. I read William Bridges's *Managing*

Transitions to prepare myself for the move to Houston. Even though I met with Steve and told him I would consider his very kind offer to match the salary promised by my new employer, the counteroffer came too late. The wave of inertia toward the other job had rolled with force I couldn't stop.

A couple weeks later, on a sunny warm mid-February day, I joined Kathleen in meeting a group of managers at the Customer Care Center in North Houston. She presented me as the new vice president, and I received a comforting welcome. After the meet and greet session, we traveled to downtown Houston to the multi-building campus. We made our way to the board room, where she introduced me to a group of executives including the president, forty-year-old Mr. Graf. I couldn't wait to hear that story.

"I would like to introduce Cal King, Vice President, Customer Care Center." A round of applause followed. It felt wonderful. Both pride and humility filled my heart as I looked around the room to many smiling faces. I don't remember seeing any other black faces. I wondered if my appointment represented another first. The new millennium had arrived, so that shouldn't have mattered. Did it?

Think fast, Cal, you need to say something. "I'm very excited to join this team. I expect to do great things here. I only have a couple regrets—I'm leaving behind snow and my beloved Indianapolis Colts!"

My brother Rod and I were rabid Colts fans. We had season tickets, and for years had never missed a home game at Indianapolis's Hoosier Dome. Even after I decided to move, I promised Rod I would still fly up for home games.

The roar of laughter, followed by chatter and teasing all around the room about weather up North and NFL teams, calmed me. *Whew, passed the first test!* The fire was back. I dusted off my career play book and started a new season. I would dazzle everyone here in the next five years, be promoted to senior vice president, and then move on to the next mountain. The quest to run a company resumed. Or so I thought.

Kathleen assigned a list of strategic projects for me to complete. I had several other tasks, which I added to her list. The call center still glowed in its infancy. The solid chassis made for a great foundation, but I felt we needed to complete the development and put on some finishing touches. My personal goal involved making this a world class contact center. She turned me loose with the help and support of Glenn, the technology director in the call center.

I had interviewed with Glenn and immediately hit it off with him. He was a brilliant and articulate man, having graduated with honors from University of Virginia. His impressive business background included holding an MBA. In addition, he played baseball in the Major League Baseball farm system.

One might think that background would make him full of himself. Nothing could be further from the truth. He exuded humility and genteel behavior to everyone he met. His soft-spoken and compromising speech hid a quiet inner strength I admired and came to rely upon.

His disposition, coupled with my charging, rah-rah style, forged a winning combination. I fired up the troops. Glenn kept me honest with explanations of the technology that would support our strategic initiatives. I had a mantra for the team. I quoted it every chance I got. "We can try a bunch of stuff. Throw it against the wall; if it sticks, great. If it doesn't, oh well, move on and try something else."

The list of accomplishments we achieved impressed onlookers. I wanted to change the name from the Customer Care Center to the Client Care Center. My explanation to Kathleen pointed out McDonald's had customers, while our account holders were valued clients receiving professional financial advice. She loved the idea, and we made it happen.

Change and transition challenged the team, but we were making great strides. There were two or three critical success factors in my mind. The first pillar of success included employee involvement. We established cross-functional working groups for every project and sent formal announcements to the entire staff about each project. They were well informed about what we were trying to do. The second pillar of success derived from complete support from Kathleen and Glenn. The third pillar consisted of my creativity, drive, and relentless determination. Having an engaging style and personal touch also helped.

Slowly but surely, the culture began to change. This took a monumental effort but was worth every minute of work. There were people to impress, so I worked untold hours the first few months. My weekdays started at 4:30 or 5:00 am. I would prepare myself for the day with a run followed by a bike ride. I'd arrive at the office by 8:00 am and sometimes work twelve hours. On the weekends, I would do a work out, get cleaned up, and hit the office by 10 am. After working to midafternoon, I'd spend a relaxing evening at home.

Chapter 7

THE "BROWN FELLAS"

The Price of Success

A TERRIBLE LONELINESS CONSUMED ME COMPLETELY during the first few months of living and working in Houston. Even though there were upward of three hundred people in my call center, and five million people in the area, I had no intimate friends or family with me. There was no one to hug, touch, or interact with. I had left behind my immediate and extended family. I also left behind the close friends on Team Fudd. That loneliness drove me to work virtually all day. I found my life slowly wobbling out of balance.

Going to Lakewood Church helped. Pastor Joel Osteen's messages of encouragement and the rousing worship lifted my spirits on Sunday mornings. However, by Sunday afternoon, I would be staring at the walls in my apartment. I tried to stay connected with my network of friends in Indiana via telephone and e-mails, but it wasn't enough.

I accepted the idea that this phase of career advancement came with the price of loneliness. I would pay this invoice in order to advance my career until I made friends in Houston. Making friends proved difficult. I worked all the time. At Lincoln Life, I'd learned I should exercise an abundance of care in developing relationships with co-workers. People had made ill-conceived assumptions about me and some of the women there. To avoid the same mistakes in Houston, I forced myself to visit museums or go to concerts alone. I also went to Astros baseball games at Enron Field. The Compaq Center was literally across the street from my apartment complex. That made going to pro basketball games very convenient. Even so, most always, I felt all alone in a crowd of thousands.

I made my home in a 975-square-foot luxury flat in a gated community on the edge of the West University section of Houston near Rice University. The world-renowned Medical Center bordered the south end of the neighborhood. Besides the Medical Center and Rice, "West U" featured an oasis of beautiful trees and perfectly landscaped homes. One could feel a wonderful vibe in this community. Lawyers, doctors, and business professionals lived and raised families in the community.

Houston is the fourth-largest city in the United States, a fact that Houstonians are proud to share. Tumbleweed didn't roll down the streets. There were no cowboys kicking dirt around, as I had expected. To the contrary, Houston sported a fast-paced, traffic-infested, vibrant metropolis.

I visited the local bike store to keep the Black Beauty finely tuned and riding smoothly. Scott and Brian weren't around. I needed someone to help me with the latest gadgets to ensure my bike maintained tip-top shape. So, the guys at the bike store helped me select great Rolf Vector Pro wheels which gave my bike a sleek look and made it lighter and faster.

Because of Houston's blast furnace heat and humidity, during the late spring and summer I spent early mornings exercising. Like many, many other fitness nuts in the area, I ran along the sycamore-tree-lined path around Rice University. I also enjoyed riding laps on my Cannondale on a makeshift cycle track on the Rice football stadium parking lot.

Virtually every morning, I loaded the Black Beauty into the back of my SUV and drove the short drive to Rice. Once there, I'd run five miles. Immediately after that workout, I unloaded my bike and rode ten miles on the track. My friend, Scott, introduced me to this type of workout. He called it a "brick." Scott, a super triathlete, competed in the Hawaiian Ironman several times. I trusted his training tips. This exercise regimen kept me physically fit and served as an outlet for the stress and strain of managing a multimillion dollar call center.

When I wasn't working out at Rice, I worked out in Memorial Park, the huge area stretching several miles between the Galleria area and downtown. Hundreds of people played and exercised in this beautiful central city haven. I did my very long weekend workouts in Memorial and along the Buffalo Bayou greenway. Although many other runners used these paths, I never joined any of them. I ran along in solitude. The camaraderie I enjoyed with Team Fudd seemed very distant.

There should have been much more to Houston life than this. Life seemed to pass me by. My days consisted of a tight and controlled regimen. I lived alone in Houston because I had been a workaholic, letting my marriage go to hell because of stubbornness. I didn't want to make it work. As a result, our nearly twenty-year union had gone down in flames destined for a 60/40 division of assets in dissolution.

The lawyers made out big-time. My emotions and feelings became more calloused than ever before. I had many positive victories in my life, but over time, I had grown further and further away from my wife. We lived a big lie in my opinion. We tried to show everyone things were fine. They weren't.

There were the fights, disagreements, and the silent withdrawals unhappy couples clothe themselves with. I gradually pulled far enough away until finally I found a way to get out. I took a job 1,200 miles from home and then made the move alone. I had turned emotional distance into physical separation. Freedom from an albatross of unhappiness had come with the price of loneliness.

I had followed in the footsteps of my Pops. We both ended up interested in women outside of marriage and then ultimately left the wife of our youths. Like my Pops, I moved far away from my children. I never knew if leaving his family made him feel as lonely, guilty, and sad as I felt about leaving mine. I never got up enough nerve to ask him. I buried myself in exercise and work in Houston to cover up those feelings.

There were some interesting characters in my apartment complex who didn't care about my past. Nor did it matter I had embarked upon a new life to jump-start a stalled career. They served as companions from time to time. I called them "Brown Fellas."

In the North, when a person has cockroaches in his home, it's usually a sign of filth or poverty. If I visited someone's home and saw a cockroach dart across the wall or floor, I would refuse to eat at his place. A "Brown Fella" sighting would also prompt checking my clothing to make sure none got into my pockets or shoes. God forbid I spend the night in a hotel or someone's home and see a roach. I would be paranoid for days that one got into my luggage, made the return trip home with me, and laid a bunch of eggs. Perhaps even took up residence.

Doc had raised a total neat freak. Some single men are natural slobs, and their apartments or houses are disgusting. Even though I lived alone, my place would pass an inspection by Mr. Clean. I laundered my clothes every day and washed and properly stored dishes after every meal. Foodstuffs were covered tightly. I organized my closets and kept my bathroom pristine. My flat was spotless, smartly decorated, and elegant. Felix from "The Odd Couple" would have been completely comfortable at my place. After all, I paid top-dollar rent for a luxury apartment in a prime Houston location. I didn't expect to see any unwelcome visitors of any kind—creepy, crawling, or otherwise. They couldn't get through the security gate unless they were granted access by a resident. All my neighbors were particular about their visitors. No soliciting took place. Roaches certainly weren't welcome!

I heard my share of roach jokes on TV. I laughed at all the stories, including roaches setting up shop, playing basketball, bowling in the cabinets. Comedians joked about roaches walking around as though they owned a place, drinking coffee, eating, or crawling around in Afros. Roaches simply gave me the creeps.

In South Texas, the story is a lot different. With the year-round warm weather, roaches thrive. They are huge. They live in trees and foliage, and they fly. I hadn't heard this news. Worst of all, they were no respecter of person, and it isn't uncommon to see them at all. Whether one lived in the Third Ward, a beautiful suburban home, a mansion, or a gated luxury apartment community in West U, chances are, there were tree roaches somewhere close by.

One night, not long after I moved into my flat, I had a midnight bladder-emptying urge. I dragged myself out of bed, slowly steadying my legs for the short journey to the bathroom. The plush carpet and rugs on my bedroom floor warmly caressed my feet as I made my way, in half stupor, onto the cool tile floor of the bathroom. *Could I do this in the dark, or should I turn on the lights?* I decided to wing it and handle my business in the dark.

"Wow. I'm thirsty. Better get a drink while I'm up," I whispered to the shadows. I kept disposable cups on the double sink vanity. I fumbled around for the cups and turned on the cold water spigot. Suddenly, something moved. I jumped and stumbled in the direction of the light switch.

I flicked the switch and glanced over at the six-foot mirror above my vanity. A Brown Fella, nearly three inches long, rested on the mirror. I began a hasty retreat! The fall backwards landed me hard into my bathtub and roused me out of my half-sleep stupor. I gathered myself in the tub and moved quickly out of the bathroom as I rubbed my head. The Brown Fella never budged, although his long antennae slowly waved during my crash landing into the bathtub. I ran to my closet to grab a shoe. Stopping to gather my courage, I slowly approached the bathroom. He was still there.

Oh, my God! What should I do? If I whack him too hard, I could break the mirror. I quickly weighed the other options. *Leave him alone and hope he leaves my apartment. Nope; not likely that would happen. Use a wad of tissue or paper towel to squish him? Nope; that's gross, and it might not work! Okay. Use the shoe.*

As I raised my shoe to deliver him to hell, he made a run for it. I whacked the mirror and missed. He jumped down on the vanity and ran faster than I thought a bug that big could run. As he scurried away, my next swat found its mark. The resulting sound was a combination squish and crunch. It took all the courage I could muster to wipe him up with a wad of tissue and flush him unceremoniously down the toilet.

My heart pounded in total panic. Roaches travel in packs. If he found his way into my bathroom, there had to be others nearby. I turned on every light in my apartment, opened all the drawers and looked behind furniture. Even though I didn't see any more Brown Fellas, the rest of the night passed without sleep.

The next morning, as soon as I thought someone would answer, I called the management office. The maintenance guy answered. I told him about my adventure with a measure of disgust. I demanded that the manager call me and that he spray my apartment immediately. The response I got unsettled me.

"How big was he?"

"What?'

"How big was he? If it was small, then we have a problem, but if it was big, then it was probably *just* a tree roach. They are everywhere and not a big problem. We'll spray just in case, but there's really nothing we can do."

"It was huge."

"Yep, tree roach. It should be alright, but like I said, we'll spray to make sure."

An hour later, the property manager told me the same thing.

A month or so later, Doc visited me, and a couple weeks after that, my brother Rod and his family came to spend a few days vacation and to visit Galveston with all its attractions. I told Doc about the Brown Fellas because I didn't want her to think all her training had been in vain. I forgot to tell Rod and his wife, Belinda.

Of course, a couple days into their visit, my niece Brittany had a similar encounter to mine, just as they were about to leave for a day trip to Moody Gardens in Galveston. Brittany spotted one of my adversaries in the bathroom. She ran out of there in sheer and utter terror, shrieking to her mom and dad.

"Uncle Calvin has roaches!" I guess she had a problem with them too.

When I came home that night, as we were leaving for a quiet dinner in Rice Village, I had to explain to Rod and Belinda that I wasn't a filthy pig, living with roaches. They were just my roommates. I apologized in total embarrassment, but they understood, and we had a big laugh about the whole thing. I promised to send a couple Brown Fellas home with them as a keepsake and a reminder of my hospitality. They declined my offer.

Those visits helped with the loneliness, but I still missed my kids terribly. Seeing Rod and his children didn't help matters at all. They seemed so happy. I lived alone with the Brown Fellas in Houston's sweltering heat. Spring had given way to midsummer 2000, and I had been simply too busy to fly to Indiana to spend time with my children, as I had promised. I missed so many important events in their lives.

My absence at games, meetings, or special events provided another source of irritation for Bernice toward me. On top of that, I had roundly rejected all her attempts to reconcile and move our family to Houston to try to make a go of it. On the other hand, I had invited my mom, Rod, and Belinda to visit me. Bernice was livid about that. This only fueled the fire that my family had been against her. What a misguided shame. It wasn't her fault. She made an earnest effort to rein me in. I resisted on every front. People in Fort Wayne gave her a hard time about letting me go, but we both knew the truth. I had proven emphatically I didn't want to work things out with her at all.

Kristi and Geoff were confused and felt as though I didn't care about them. Nothing was further from the truth. I loved them with all my heart. I separated from them only because I wanted to start a new life without their mom. I was attempting to make a name for myself professionally and stop living a life of lies and wandering eyes. I hadn't been happy in marriage for years. Things were not going to work out the way they wanted, because I didn't want them to. They didn't understand the distinction about how I felt about them, and how I felt about the marriage. The relationships were fundamentally different. Little did I know, as much as I would hate it, in a short while, their mom would be in charge of my every move. I would be able to do nothing about it.

Part II
THE INVISIBLE FORCE

Chapter 8

CHICAGO, CHICAGO, THAT TODDLING TOWN

A Deadly Business Trip

EACH YEAR, CALL CENTER PROFESSIONALS FROM all over North America gather for the International Call Center Management Conference and Exposition. The twelfth annual event in Chicago's McCormick Place, at the beginning of August 2000, drew an audience of 1,500 attendees. They were all dedicated to keeping up-to-date with the management practices and implementation of call center solutions for the new millennium's competitive business environment. Glenn and I looked forward to accessing expert speakers, networking opportunities, and a chance to attend in-depth sessions. The presenters were leading suppliers of call center products and services. Steve Forbes was scheduled to deliver the keynote presentation. His appearance piqued my interest. I thought his bid for the presidency had a fighting chance until the wheels fell off. I wanted to hear his speech.

Chicago had long been one of my favorite cities. I had fond memories of Gramps and Mama Lucy and their life on the West Side years past. Although I hadn't been near their neighborhood since they died, I had been a huge Cubs fan for years. As such, I made trips to Wrigley Field to watch games almost every summer. The North Side of town seemed a world away from the West Side and the sprawling South Side where my uncles and cousins still lived.

My days of business travel had essentially ended with moving out of the commercial real estate investment analyst role. I longed to travel on a company's dime. I had been working hard and felt as though I deserved a boondoggle, while networking and picking up call center knowledge. Where better to do that than on Michigan Avenue? A jaunt to the Magnificent Mile in Chicago, with a few trips to the McCormick Place convention center, would do the trick.

This trip also presented an opportunity to get back to the Midwest. It would be an escape from the blast furnace heat and humidity of the Gulf Coast. I had a hard time adjusting to the summer weather in Houston. I discovered that people in the North stay inside during the winter and enjoy outdoor activities in spring and summer. Houston outdoor activity life presented the opposite scenario. People tried to stay indoors during the summer but thoroughly enjoyed the outdoors in fall, winter, and spring.

In the back of my mind, I thought there might be a chance to sneak in a trip to Fort Wayne to see some friends and Kris and Geoff. After all, driving to Fort Wayne would be an easy trip—I could get there in three hours from Chicago.

I missed my kids terribly. I considered a couple options to see them. I could fly them to Houston the second week of August, or I could make the short drive over to Fort Wayne from Chicago. However, the more I looked at the schedule of events for the conference, the more I realized it would be nearly impossible to break way. That left only one thing to do: call Bernice and ask her to let the kids come down to Houston for a visit.

That idea went over like a lead balloon and started a fresh round of heated discussions. The wounds of our marriage battles were still too fresh and painful. Incredibly, running that gauntlet paid off. In the end, she agreed to let the kids fly down the second week in August. I immediately made the reservations. My confidant and trusted administrative assistant, Lois, also made arrangements for Glenn and me to travel to Chicago on August 1. She cleared my calendar, as much as she could, the second week of August.

The week before we left for Chi-town, Lois sat with me to go over the travel plans and accommodations for the ICCM conference. Unfortunately, all of the rooms were taken in the hotel chains I recognized. The only rooms left were in a hotel a couple blocks off Michigan Avenue. I'd never heard of it, but it was too late to do anything about it. Besides, I couldn't concentrate on those details. I could hardly contain my pure excitement about another NFL preseason starting that weekend. Time for me to check out my Colts! The Indianapolis team was playing the Atlanta Falcons. Most of all, this would be a great time bonding with Rod—my baby brother and best friend. We left every contest hoarse and exhilarated. I had no earthly idea I would only see one more game that season. I wouldn't be cheering loudly with the others when I returned.

The following Tuesday, Glenn and I made the direct flight to O'Hare International Airport and caught a cab down to the Gold Coast. Each day of the conference, we hailed a taxi and were whisked from our North Michigan Avenue area hotel over to Lake Shore Drive and south to beautiful McCormick Place. The skyline and Lake Michigan were breathtaking. My eyes drank in the beauty of downtown Chicago. I saw runners along the beach off Lake

Shore Drive. This made me glad about my decision to bring running shoes. I couldn't wait to get out for a long, relaxing run to see the city skyline from the running path on the lakefront.

The excitement of walking up and down Rush Street in the evenings grabbed me. Rush Street offered some fine night life and appealed to yuppies like Glenn and me. More than anything else, I anxiously looked forward to dinner in the famous Pump Room. The Pump Room—on State Street in the Ambassador East Hotel—opened in 1938 and became a magnet for movie stars and celebrities. For years, it was a highly acclaimed restaurant and Chicago landmark. When Glenn and I made the short walk from our hotel for dinner, the Pump Room remained a place for stargazing. As we entered the lobby, we caught a glimpse of Steven Spielberg. I nudged Glenn in the side with glee. I'd seen a star!

On the last day of the three-day conference, I got up early to get on my running gear. If I missed exercising this morning, I would break my string of running in every city I visited. The sun shined brilliantly. A gentle breeze cut through the blue, cloudless sky. This day would be a perfect setting for a five- or six-mile run before breakfast. I left my hotel room clad in running gear, got on the elevator, and strode through the lobby. After stepping onto the busy sidewalk, I ran a half mile or so east across North Michigan Avenue toward Lake Shore Drive. The morning air felt crisp and clean. I approached the entryway to an underpass at Lake Shore to the Lake Michigan waterfront in full stride.

A stale smell of garbage and urine smacked me in the face. I nearly tripped over a homeless man as I strode into the tunnel on my way toward the waterfront. Despite that obstacle, I found myself on the running path near the edge of the lake. For a few seconds, I wondered if there were other, less seedy entryways across Lake Shore.

After a left turn, I headed up the coast and picked up speed. The wind moved briskly at the waterfront. Many people think Chicago is called the Windy City because of the wind. Truth is it gained notoriety due to crooked politicians who brokered deals in smoky backrooms, many years ago. It's actually known as the Windy City because those same city politicians used to give long-winded speeches at city hall. That morning, I didn't care about politicians and windy speeches. Mother Nature's wind blew mists of water from Lake Michigan directly into me. After awhile, this mist felt wonderfully refreshing, so I inhaled several wisps from the great lake as I settled into a comfortable pace.

I trotted a few miles up the beach, well past Northwestern University to the edge of the residential areas on the north side of town. What fantastic views! Lake Michigan displayed its blue splendor on my right, and the metropolitan

Chicago skyline rose majestically to my left. Sweat poured out of me as I made my way back south toward Ohio Street. All the while, I hummed a tune I'd learned many years ago:

> *Chicago, Chicago, that toddling town*
> *Chicago, Chicago, I will show you around,—I love it*
> *Bet your bottom dollar you lose the blues in Chicago, Chicago*

What a great song. It kept me moving until I came up to the rank-smelling tunnel underneath Lake Shore on my route back to the Magnificent Mile. I ran through this stinky passageway as quickly as I could but still inhaled moist air. I kept a careful eye for the homeless man I'd seen there an hour ago.

By midafternoon August 3, we were back at O'Hare for our flight to Houston. I enjoyed this trip, but I eagerly awaited the flight home. I had met a new friend who would be a huge part of my life in the days ahead. Shortly after the plane landed, I joined Michele and her aunt Lynn for dinner.

I met Michele a couple months before at work. She took it upon herself to show me some of the sights and points of interests of Houston. She had relocated from Michigan with her two young boys a couple years earlier. Her tall, angular body and striking beauty captivated me. We both enjoyed a rigorous physical fitness regimen, although she did a better job of maintaining a proper diet than I did. We worked out and had dinner a few times. I had finally found someone who liked to work out as much as I did. Her energy and lightening-quick wit made hanging out with her a total blast during the last month. The innocent fun helped us hit it off really well. I liked her. This scared me, because I had promised myself to steer clear of relationships. I wanted to stay focused on my work. Michele had just ended a long relationship and wasn't really trying to start anything serious either. We had fun together but had a good understanding about our friendship. Still, I found myself smitten by her. She helped drive away the loneliness that had gripped me in its clutches during midsummer. I couldn't stop thinking about her.

Friendly bantering and giggling went on the entire dinner. I enjoyed their company, although I wasn't feeling all that well and couldn't eat much. The Houston heat sweltered that night, but I felt chilled and tired. I figured the jet lag and rigors of back-to-back trips to Indy and Chicago had simply worn me out. The ladies bid me goodnight with an embrace.

"Cal, you don't look so good." Michele said. She touched my forehead. "Man, you feel warm. Maybe you should go home and get some rest. You might want to skip working out tomorrow too."

That sounded like a great idea. The last thing I needed was to be sick when

Kris and Geoff got to Houston. "I will. Take care. Call me this weekend, if you have a chance."

"Okay, I will. Take care!"

"Bye, Cal. It was great meeting you." Lynn flashed a warm smile. I knew I had passed muster.

"It was good meeting you too, Lynn. Keep this one out of trouble." I said, pointing toward Michele, who stuck out her tongue and crossed her eyes. I wouldn't see Michele again for months. It wasn't because I didn't want to. I could spend every day with her. In just a few weeks time, I had fallen for her, but I was about to embark upon a long journey I would have to walk primarily alone.

I wasn't one to get sick. On the rare occasions I did get the sniffles or sore throat, I typically toughed it out. Usually I'd go on runs to sweat the sickness out. That trick didn't seem to work with this cold. I called my mama to see if she had any suggestions or home remedies. I didn't want her to worry about me, so I played the whole thing off.

"Hey, Doc! What's going on?"

"CK! Nothing much, baby. What's going on down there?"

"Just relaxing and trying to keep cool. Man, it's so hot down here. Getting ready for Kristi and Geoff to come down, you know. They will be here Tuesday, so I had to make sure I had some food in the place."

"That's wonderful. I know you're glad they're coming down. I know you ain't cooking, are you? Take them to Pappadeaux's, where we went." Doc loved fried catfish. I had taken her there when she visited me. She knew I wasn't going to cook because when she visited, I didn't have many pots, pans, or utensils for cooking. Doc insisted on going to the store to buy a set of cookware for me. It was a kind gesture, but those things weren't getting much use at all.

"Yeah, I'm hoping to have some fun with them, but I don't plan on doing any cooking, that's for sure. It's too hot. Too many good restaurants down here. Besides, those kids won't want to be all cooped up in this tiny apartment, Doc. I had to fight with Bernice to let them come. She wanted to come with them, but I said no. That didn't go over well at all. I just want to spend time with them and hang out before they start school in a couple weeks. I'll probably take a couple days off work while they're here. I'm thinking about taking them to a basketball game and maybe the movies. Remember that huge theater I showed you when you came down?"

"CK, sounds like you coming down with something."

"Aw, Doc, it's just a little cold. No big deal. I'll take something."

"Take you some Tylenol and pump fluids. Get you some rest. You probably down there workin' too hard."

I knew she would tell me to take it easy, but I'd gotten her recommendation. "I'm fine, Mom. Don't worry about me. Take care of yourself. I'll call you in a couple days."

Finally, Tuesday afternoon came. I rushed to Hobby Airport to pick up Kristi and Geoffrey. I waited at the gate nervously and then, there they were! Kristi came out first. She flashed a big smile as I ran toward her. Geoffrey followed, but he glowered and frowned. His face said, "You hurt my mom's feelings. This is weird." I grabbed him and hugged them both as tight as I could. It was a gargantuan group hug. I literally willed a smile to Geoff's face.

"I love you guys so much. I miss you!"

"I love you too, Daddy." Kristi said.

Geoff followed with an "I love you," and a bear hug.

The party was on after that. We had to make up for lost time. We were all over the place the rest of the week. We shopped nonstop. I spent hundreds of dollars on school clothes. We took in a WNBA Comets game. We saw a movie at the theater near my house. The kids enjoyed the pool and the other amenities at my apartment complex. I worked half days the first two days as they slept in. I tried to be alert and attentive every minute I shared with them. I didn't call Michele or contact any other friends. I wanted to give Kris and Geoff my undivided attention, all the while wishing I felt better and trying my best to hide my misery from them.

Kristi and I had long discussions on my patio late into the evenings. We had been very close over the years. She looked to her dad for guidance on so many issues. It was clear she missed our long, and sometimes deep, conversations.

"Dad, I just don't understand why you are down here all alone."

I tried to explain why I lived in Houston, while they were still in Indiana. There was no way I could convince her that the situation felt right.

By Thursday afternoon, my body felt feverish. I wasn't eating. Even so, I had a luncheon scheduled with a vendor. I planned to go home to hang out with the kids. Lois cancelled the lunch meeting. She said I looked terrible and should go on home. I had been walking around in a daze all morning, carrying bottles of Gatorade but not drinking.

The cold got progressively worse. I drove toward home but stopped at a drugstore near my apartment and bought three or four different types of cold relief medicine. I took it all and laid down for a nap. Later that night, the kids and I grabbed a bite and went to the movies. The temperatures hovered in the midnineties, but I had been shivering all day. I had a persistent fever, vomiting, and diarrhea. I took multiple cold showers to help drive the fever down and drank bottles of Gatorade. Nothing worked.

The next day, Friday, August 11, I didn't go to work. I stayed in bed virtually all day. The kids made themselves busy. They had learned their way around West U. They commandeered my SUV and were comfortable coming and going by that time. I burned up with fever and grew very weak. By Friday evening, Kristi had grown very concerned. She talked me into going to the emergency room.

I vaguely remember her driving me to St. Luke's Hospital in the Medical Center. We waited in the emergency room lobby for a long time. All the while, I trembled violently and barked deep coughs. Finally, we were led to a small examination room. I sat in a chair in the corner of the room, and the kids waited with me. After a nurse took my vitals and left, a physician came in the room. He stood just inside the door and started talking, clipboard in hand. All the while, he never stepped towards me. He refused to cross an invisible line.

"You've got the flu." He recommended that I buy some over the counter medicine, drink fluids and rest.

What a bizarre scene. No doctor had ever exhibited this kind of bedside manner with me. He never came near me, not to listen to my heart, chest, or back. He neglected to look at my throat, ears, or nose. I felt absolutely awful. This guy never touched me and sent me back home!

Chapter 9
IT ALL STARTED IN PHILADELPHIA

The Birthplace of Legionnaire's Disease

I'D BEEN TO PHILLY A FEW times to look at commercial real estate. Mortgage bankers showed me the impressive Center City and drove me through the Main Line, the home of the well-heeled Philadelphians. We drove around Delaware County and Bucks County to find a deal suitable for Lincoln's stringent investment standards. Although the city impressed me, I never closed an investment deal there.

In 1998 the chairman and CEO of Lincoln National Corporation retired. His successor obviously had visited Philly too, because he decided to move corporate headquarters from Fort Wayne to Philadelphia shortly after he took over the reins of LNC. This relocation sent shock waves through Fort Wayne. Lincoln had been an influential corporate citizen there for decades. Its corporate officers had served on boards and been leaders in the community. As hard as it was to believe, slowly but surely, most of the corporate center staff, including my friend Dawn, moved to Philadelphia.

I hated to see her go. After the discontinuity project, we stayed in touch. She always supported me, and we had become close friends. I met Dawn during her frequent smoke breaks, and we would walk around outside the corporate headquarters building, talking about moves the company made, our families, and our work. Sometimes, we would grab lunch or meet for drinks with other project team members or friends after hours. She worried about the upcoming move to Philadelphia. Eventually, she found a place in the suburbs of Philly, made the move with one of her children, and started to adjust to her new life.

After the corporate offices moved to Philadelphia, I had to travel there for meetings a couple times during spring 1999. Reconnecting with my friends felt wonderful. Dawn eagerly suggested I see her place. So after work, we walked to Suburban Station and took the train to Berwyn, a suburb on the

Main Line. Her home felt comfortable and far from the hustle and bustle of Center City. We met four of her girlfriends for dinner and drinks.

What a fun evening. I flirted with her friends. We all laughed and drank for a couple hours. When we broke up, Dawn drove me back to the train stop and got me on a train to the city so I could get to my hotel and crash. I made it to Center City long before midnight. I decided to walk around and take in some sights. Before long, I found myself on South Broad Street walking past the Park Hyatt Philadelphia at the Bellevue, just a few blocks from Lincoln's corporate headquarters. What a stunning building!

A few years earlier, this building was known as The Bellevue-Stratford Hotel. When built in 1904, the hotel stood as the most luxurious hotel in the country. It featured amazing ballrooms, over one thousand guest rooms, light fixtures designed by Thomas Edison, plenty of marble, and a stunning elliptical staircase.

For years after its construction, the Bellevue-Stratford served as a centerpiece of Philadelphia's activities for business and wealthy individuals. There were parties, weddings, and other events held in the grand ballrooms. Several U.S. presidents and foreign dignitaries stayed at the hotel in its prime. It boasted a majestic appearance during its heyday and maintained its grand stature that night as I walked by in the cool spring evening.

What I didn't know was, twenty three years earlier, in July 1976 about 4,400 members of the American Legion were in Philadelphia to attend their annual convention as well as to celebrate our country's two-hundredth birthday. Several hundred of them stayed and or attended meetings at the Bellevue-Stratford.

A few days after the convention started, some of the Legionnaires got sick. They all had similar symptoms: fever, coughing, and difficulty breathing. No one seemed to notice. However, four days after the convention, one by one, the American Legionnaires start dying of a mysterious illness. All in all, over two hundred people got sick and thirty-four had died, many of which had either been inside the Bellevue-Stratford Hotel or had walked past it just as I had.

Nearly six months after the outbreak, the Center for Disease Control shared its findings about the deaths. The mysterious sickness was caused by bacteria that led to acute respiratory infection resulting in serious cases of pneumonia. The CDC learned the bacteria that made the Legionnaires sick could be commonly found in nature, wherever warm and moist stagnant water pooled. The bacteria transmitted to people by them breathing it deep into their lungs.

Eventually, experts determined that the bacteria, called *Legionella,* resided in the water of cooling towers of the hotel. The CDC believed the Legionnaire's disease bacteria actually spread by way of the air-conditioning systems via water droplets. People who inhaled the aerosols inevitably inhaled the microorganisms into their respiratory tracts, causing flu-like symptoms, confusion, and, where untreated, pneumonia that resulted in death.

In addition, research found that the Legionnaire's disease bacteria bred unchecked in natural freshwater sources. Once the bacteria were identified, scientists determined there had been other previously unresolved outbreaks. Most of the cases seem to occur sporadically. The risk factors for contracting Legionnaire's disease depended on the health of the victim or the number of *Legionellae* that reached the body. People who smoke, drank, or who had weakened immune systems were especially susceptible to the effects of the disease.

People stricken with Legionnaire's disease can survive. Mortality rates vary. However, those who survive may suffer from long-term side effects. The most common side effects are fatigue and lack of energy. There are some other rare and life-changing side effects I would learn about and experience firsthand later on.

I marveled at the Bellevue-Stratford and Center City skyline for a while longer before heading back to my hotel, never realizing the deadly history made there.

Chapter 10
THE TUNNEL, THE BAKERY, AND VIETNAM

In the Clutches of a Rare Disease

I HAD BEEN DEEMED UNTOUCHABLE BY the emergency room doctor, and sent home to recover with the aid of over-the-counter medicine. Maybe there had been a flu outbreak. Perhaps nothing on my chart screamed out that something strange and terrible had happened to me. Maybe the doctor neared the end of a long shift, just wanted to get through the last few patients, and get the heck out of there. Maybe he didn't think the flu-like symptoms I presented with were a real emergency. He just wanted to move on to the real emergencies. After all, the emergency room teemed with sick people that night. Whatever his reasons were, clearly I had to leave there that night with no treatment.

Kristi and Geoffrey were perplexed and angry with the doctor, because they knew I wasn't getting any better. They had thoroughly explained all the symptoms to the nurse and the people in triage. In the end, all they could do was load me into the SUV and make the short drive home.

The harsh coughing from the depths of my chest continued throughout that night and into the next morning of Saturday, August 12. The rest of that day, a battle loomed for me. Later, Kristi would tell me that day was the worst day of her life. The kids never left the apartment. Instead, they kept themselves busy listening to music and watching television as they checked on me throughout the afternoon. They gave me cold and flu medicine I'd bought from Walgreens a couple days prior. My fever raged, and I shivered. I kept trying to drink, but I had I vomited so much that by midafternoon, all I could do was dry heave. My lips were cracked from dehydration, but I had ceased to attempt to take in fluids. The coughing grew progressively worse. It continued with more and more fervor.

The phone rang a few times. I heard Kristi politely tell callers about my sickness and explain I couldn't come to the phone. Michele called to check on me since I hadn't called her as promised. She had grown concerned about how I looked a few nights before. We typically talked every day, so she knew something was going on with me. I couldn't work out or meet her for dinner though. She certainly would understand. I really had no idea who else called or if Kristi phoned her mom for instructions on how to care for me. I didn't want her to do that, but I couldn't prevent her from doing so.

There were new problems developing for me. Each time I got up to go to the bathroom, the room spun around and around. Dizziness gripped me, I staggered and nearly fell. Geoffrey helped me get to the bathroom. The sounds of the television in my living room became more and more muffled and faint. I couldn't tell if I was dreaming or awake. My mind played tricks on me, as I faded in and out of a blackness I'd never experienced before. It felt as though I walked into a very long tunnel to an all-enveloping darkness. I could make out Kristi's face close to mine, but I couldn't understand what she said to me all the time.

The afternoon seemed to drag on for an eternity. As hard as I tried to move myself back to wellness, it didn't work. All I could do was lie in my bed. By early evening, I tried to move my arms and legs, but they wouldn't respond.

"Dad, are you okay?" Kristi asked.

I whispered faintly. "I can't move, baby. I feel awful."

Geoff had a plan. "Let's take him back to the emergency room. Is that okay with you, Dad?"

I nodded. Although they were standing over me, it felt has though I returned their concerned and frightened stares from a great distance. Their voices were a distant chant I could barely hear or understand.

"Kristi, we can't move him, he's too out of it. Let's call EMS."

"Dad, we're calling the EMS to come and take you to the hospital."

Questions floated in my mind. What if the same doctor was there? He'd just send me back here. Am I going to die? If so, where is the bright light I've heard about when death nears? What should I do? How will the ambulance get past the front gate?

"You'll have to let them in the front gate. The bright light has to get through too." I wasn't sure if I said this or just thought it. Confusion engulfed my mind. I floated off to the blackness of the tunnel. It had returned with a new density.

I awakened to several men standing over me in my bedroom. They were taking my vital signs and asking me questions. Surely I dreamt. I couldn't respond, and I couldn't move. They all looked serious and worked quickly and silently. Before I knew it, they had placed me on a stretcher and we were in the hot Houston August night air.

"Kristi, get my briefcase."

The blackness parted, and I saw the bright lights of a hospital room. I rested in complete and utter stillness on a stretcher covered in white sheets. My eyes moved and drank in the surroundings as I stared up and down the long, sterile, gray walls. A quiet coolness permeated the room. My arms and legs had a mind of their own and refused to follow my commands.

"Where am I?"

"Your dad is really sick," the doctor explained to Kris and Geoff. The three of them stood over me. "This is an x-ray of his chest." He held the x-ray film up so the lights would show the image. "See all this white coloring in his lungs? It's infection."

I tried to nod and join in on the discussion, but no one seemed to notice.

"It looks as though he has pneumonia."

Ah ha! That's why I am so sick….now let's get this show on the road. Give me a shot, and get me out of here! No one heard me.

"We're going to admit him." He touched my arm. "We'll take care of your dad."

The blackness returned. I tried my best to push it back, but the uselessness of that effort overcame my will to find light.

I shopped at two grocery stores: Kroger and Randalls. Kroger backed right up behind my apartment complex while Randalls could be reached by virtue of a short drive of less than a mile. Even though Kroger offered convenience because of its proximity, I often drove to Randalls because it had an in-store bank branch. I had opened accounts at the branch when I moved to Houston, and I used the in-store ATM. One of the customer service employees there was a drop-dead gorgeous brunette. I loved going there to stare at her while I waited in line to conduct my business. The post office and several popular retail stores were also in the Randalls strip center. This made it easy to handle numerous errands with virtually one stop. The weather was sunny, warm, and perfect for a drive, so I decided to head for Randalls.

Today, the trophy would be in bakery items. Yummy, the hunt began! The bakery displayed cakes, cookies, and more pies than I'd ever seen. A virtual wonderland of confectionary delights and baked goods paraded before me. My mind drifted back to all of the treats Doc lovingly made from scratch, nearly every Sunday. This presentation rivaled all the things she baked except for her lemon meringue pie. I wistfully wished for a huge slice, so I started to search the racks and shelves.

Items were neatly displayed on half a dozen tables. Each table beckoned me, but none could fulfill the quest for the holy meringue pie.

Behind the glass cases, near the back of the bakery section, a group of women dressed in black trousers, black polo shirts, white aprons, and hats faced me. They were covered with flour from whipping up scrumptious delights all morning. They all watched me closely, smiled, and nodded.

"Can we help you, sir?"

"Sure. I'm looking for a lemon meringue pie. Do ya'll have any?"

It was a simple question, but I couldn't seem to get an answer. They whispered among themselves while occasionally glancing over at me. A couple more women emerged from the back room and joined in the discussion. I leaned up against the glass case and tried to listen to the conversation.

"It *is* him," one of the ladies whispered.

This was getting ridiculous. "Excuse me! Ladies, do you have lemon meringue pie?" *What the hell? How hard could this be? Either they have the pie, or they don't. If they don't have it, then I'm going over to Kroger.* "It's no big deal. If you don't have it, no big deal…"

The short one, with big brown eyes, broke away from the group and walked over to the counter. The other flour-clad bakers watched her closely as if to guide her through the impending exchange. She leaned over the case and beckoned me closer, as if to tell me a secret. She whispered in broken English laden with a heavy Spanish accent.

"Sir, you follow me for 'leeemon' pie."

"What?"

She beckoned me around the glass counter. I nervously followed her, but the urge for the pie grew stronger than my apprehension about going into the back room. The gallery of bakers parted as Brown Eyes led me to the prize. As we entered the kitchen, I looked around. A fine mist of flour powder floated in the air. It covered the floors, the shelves, the heavy duty baking equipment and the ovens. I coughed after inhaling a powdery mist deep into my lungs. A white wooden chair sat in the middle of the room. It seemed out of place there, where obviously people worked with equipment to produce the goodies out front.

I no more than stepped through the threshold of the door, when someone grabbed me from behind and held me in a strong bear hug. I felt myself being lifted up and slammed hard to the floor. My face landed in a clump of flour. Before I could move, there were kicks from black boots into my torso. All of the air left my body. I lay limp, covered in flour. I tried to yell for help, but the kicking resumed. I moaned in agony.

Two big men dressed in white bakery attire, lifted me from the floor and shoved me into the chair. One of them strode over to the door and slammed it shut in one swift motion.

"Get the rope!" he said to his partner.

"Right, hold him down while I tie him up."

They bound my hands behind the back of the chair. My legs were bound to the front chair legs. Several strands of thick rope wrapped around my torso, holding me in place. No escape route presented itself for me. After binding me, the flour boys stepped back to admire their handy work. I meekly looked up through puffy eyes. They glared at me.

"Now, get the racks." Soon, empty racks used to hold loaves of bread stacked neatly on either side of me. Their work finished, the men left and slammed the door. I heard a deadbolt clink solidly into place.

Hours passed, but no one came to save me. I tried to yell for help, but each time I opened my mouth to scream, I coughed up flour. The heavy white mist enveloped me until I was covered in flour from head to toe. Kathleen would be looking for me. Staff meeting had started, and I would be late if I didn't get out of here. I wanted to call her to tell her I had been held captive and needed her help.

All of a sudden, the deadbolt clicked, and the door cracked open. Someone stepped into the room, followed by the two men who beat and bound me to the chair. A strange-looking woman strode towards me.

"Let me go!"

She laughed wickedly. "Take him away."

Immediately, one of the men crossed to the back of the room to open a thick grey metal door. I shook as hard as I could to try to break free as the men lifted me from the floor, still bound to the chair. They carried me through the door, down a ramp, into a waiting box truck. An automatic lift raised me to the bed of the vehicle. The bakery boys shoved me unceremoniously into the back of the big white box truck.

As soon as the door latch clicked, the big truck pulled off and drove me to a large bakery warehouse several blocks away. The boys unloaded me and placed me into a small storage room. I struggled with all my might but could not break free.

A couple days had passed since Kristi and Geoffrey called the ambulance to take me to St. Luke's Episcopal Hospital. Some of the finest doctors and medical professionals in the country practiced there. None of that mattered to me because of my total state of confusion. I pulled off wires, oxygen masks, and barked at the staff. Let the combat begin.

Kristi had called her mom. She and Geoff were overwhelmed with my condition. Bernice dropped everything and caught the first available plane to Houston. Once the red-eye flight landed and she got settled in at St. Luke's, she called Rod in the wee hours of the morning to tell him about my hospitalization. Although I hadn't treated her very well since deciding to leave her several months before, this situation presented an opportunity for her to show that she still cared for me, even though things had been bad between us. She unselfishly put her strong Christian values ahead of all the problems.

"Is he always this stubborn?' the nurse asked. She tried to put a cup to my mouth again, but I clenched my lips shut, and turned my head.

"Yes, he's pretty stubborn. Calvin, let her give you some medicine. Let her help you."

I turned my head and tried to move away. I couldn't move, so I grunted, "Leave me alone! What are *you* doing here?"

Darkness covered the room, but I wasn't in the black tunnel now. Clearly, I lay in a hospital bed. I shivered. I could tell my fever persisted. There were wires and monitors everywhere. They were trying to hurt me and no one appeared to help at all.

"Calvin, these people want to help you, and you won't let them. Please let them help you."

"No. Leave me alone." *Where is Kathleen? She can help me. I'm late for a staff meeting.*

This pleading went on and on. Finally Bernice said, "If Kathleen says it is okay for them to treat you, will you let them do it?"

I nodded.

She immediately grabbed a phone not far from the bed. She fumbled around in her purse and finally retrieved the paper she was looking for. She purposely dialed a number and began to talk in muffled tones. *What did she say?* After a few minutes, she put the receiver to my ear.

"Hi, Cal, this is Kathleen." I recognized her voice immediately and calmed down. "Cal, you're pretty sick. You need to let them take care of you."

"Is it all right? They have me strapped down in the bakery."

"It's okay. Let them help you, Cal."

"Alright."

From that moment, there seemed to be a whirlwind around me. Nurses began to draw blood from the protruding veins in my arms and administer oxygen. I had not found a doctor in Houston yet, so St. Luke's had assigned a young physician to treat me, Dr. Tuan "Mark" Tran. The staff had admitted me to the intensive care unit and begun treatment for pneumonia. A high fever persisted several days. My lungs were full of infection. Although Dr. Tran administered a combination of antibiotics to treat the pneumonia, he and his colleagues were baffled with my condition. There had been no improvement.

The trips to the Randalls bakery via the black tunnel became more and more frequent. While I was tied up in the warehouse bakery, family and friends in Indiana tried to figure out what was happening with me. Rod called Mom.

"Doc, Bernice called me last night and told me Calvin is in the hospital. I was half-asleep. I can't remember what she said. She is already in Houston. I'm not sure where she was calling me from."

"Check the caller ID, and see if there's a number, Rod."

The number belonged to a phone in the intensive care family waiting area at St Luke's. Rod called the number, and Bernice filled him in on my condition. It wasn't good. The fever wouldn't break, delirium reigned. Later that day, Doc called the hospital. She was connected to my room. Amazingly, I answered the phone. She couldn't understand a word I said. While she tried to make sense of what I said, a nurse walked in and gently took the phone from me.

"Hello. Mr. King is not supposed to be on the phone. Who is this calling?"

"This is his mother calling from Indiana. Please tell me what's going on with him."

"He's in intensive care and on full oxygen. He's not speaking clearly."

"What? I just talked to him a couple days ago. He was fine. Just a bit of a cold. What's going on down there?" Doc was distraught. Her firstborn, the special one, her golden child was in trouble. She was helpless and out of the loop.

"Someone has to go down there to find out what's going on, Rod. I need a couple days to handle affairs. Can you get down there now?"

"Sure, Doc. I'll be on a plane as soon as I can."

Within a few hours, Rod stood at my bedside. That was August 16, two days before his thirty-fourth birthday. He would be there for the next several days, sleeping in my hospital room, only leaving for meals or trips to my apartment for showers. I had many "best" friends throughout my life but no one closer to me than my little brother. Over the years, we'd grown closer and closer. We talked on the phone almost every day, sharing hopes, challenges, and jokes. We discussed our parents, our kids, and of course, Colts football. His career had taken off just like mine. I served as his mentor and tried to teach him everything I could about being a leader and an executive. I frequently buzzed down to Indy to hang out with him. Now, in the time of my big trouble, he tried to rescue me.

Miraculously, even though I had been incoherent since before arriving at St. Luke's, I recognized Rod and talked to him. I had a few messages for him. So when he leaned over my bed, I grabbed his shirt and pulled him close to my face. My voice seemed to be leaving me, and I could only whisper with great effort.

"Rod."

"Hey, dude, how you feeling?"

"Come closer. Tell Bernice to go home. I don't want her here."

"No, I think she needs to be here, Calvin."

"Send her home. Please."

"She needs to be here. It's okay. I'm here too." He had no idea how rough things had been between Bernice and me. I never discussed my marriage relationship with him, even after I moved away to Houston.

I lost the battle. "I need you to do some things for me then."

"Okay. What?"

"Go to my apartment. There's a wooden box on the shelves in my bedroom." I collected decorative wooden boxes. This one contained some very important documents and wasn't on display with the others. "My checkbook is in there. Get it and keep it. Okay?"

"Okay."

I struggled for breath and had to rest. Rod started to pull away, but I grabbed his shirt again. It was bizarre. Up until then, moving my extremities had been nearly impossible.

"Get my briefcase. There's a black day-planner in there. I need you to get that and call some people for me." I felt myself drifting off. I shared some instructions with him but wasn't quite sure what I had asked him to do. Another trip to the tunnel…

Rod shoved off to find the doctor. He was determined to learn my prognosis. He learned next to nothing. The doctors had ordered tests but still didn't know what sickness afflicted me.

Rod and Bernice watched me like hawks. The night before Rod got there, one of the employees from the call center showed up at my room in the intensive care area. It wasn't a good scene. I appeared totally incoherent and writhed in disorientation. On top of that, unbeknownst to me, I had been repeatedly calling Michele to help me. She could hear the medical monitors in the background and my labored breath. I never uttered a word during any of the calls.

Bernice put a stop to all this. She called Lois and left strict orders that I could have no visitors. Lois got the word out. This sparked rumors at the call center. People were left to imagine all sorts of things about what ailment had befallen me. There were rumors that I had a nervous breakdown caused by the pressures of the job. Some people perpetuated a rumor that I had AIDS. Of course, neither rumor was true. I loved my work and never backed down from a challenge. Furthermore, I never led a lifestyle that might lead to AIDS, nor had I been exposed to HIV by virtue of a blood transfusion. I had pneumonia, and I lived in a black tunnel.

Rod loomed at my bedside again. He smiled widely. A beautiful, short woman with olive skin, long flowing brown hair, and big brown eyes framed by wire-rimmed glasses, stood next to him.

"Mr. King, how are you? I'm Dr. Tiwari. Do you know who this is?" She had a pleasant smile and moved closer when she detected I had some difficulty answering.

"It's my brother, Rod," my voice barely a whisper. "It's his birthday"

Rod's grin got wider.

"Do you know where you are?"

"Randalls." Dr. Tiwari smiled and looked at Rod.

"What's Randalls?" he asked, totally perplexed.

The doctor chuckled. "It's a local supermarket chain."

Dr. Tran had called in Dr. Pinky Tiwari, a neurologist also on the medical staff of St. Luke's. Dr. Tiwari treated patients with disorders of the nervous system, including the brain, spinal cord, and nerves. My persistent fever had resulted in swelling of the cerebellum, and thus the need for Dr. Tiwari's expertise. They had also called in Dr. Marcia Kielhofner whose area of specialty was infectious diseases. Up until then, no one could figure out what afflicted me. The team of doctors grew more and more worried as my condition worsened day after day. Additional tests were ordered, and there were daily meetings to discuss the diagnosis.

Rod called Doc to provide an update.

"Doc, do you really want to know what's going on with Calvin?"

"Of course I do."

"Do you really want to know?"

"Roderick!"

"Mom, Calvin is in bad shape. He's totally out of it. He has no idea where he is. He doesn't know anything, except that he has a little brother. He doesn't remember Linda and Carla. He told these people he doesn't have any sisters. His motor skills are shot. He's barely able to move. And…they don't know what's wrong with him. You need to get down here, now! Doc, he might not make it. They said it's 'touch and go' over the next twenty-four hours." He cried uncontrollably. His best friend and the rock of the family hovered near death before his very eyes, and he couldn't do anything about it. His beloved hero, Calvin, would probably die, on his birthday.

Ken was my favorite restaurant manager when I worked at Lucky Steer. I had only worked with him a short while in 1971 before the Army drafted him and ultimately sent him to Vietnam to fight in the undeclared war. The images from Vietnam had been on the evening news every day for several years. The appalling scenes scared me. I felt certain I would be drafted and sent there upon high school graduation. When Ken returned from Vietnam, he frequently held court, sharing some gruesome war stories. He had changed from the laid-back, happy-go-lucky guy he was before shipping out. He had become a more serious man, with strong opinions about our country and its policies. He had seen men die for a cause he didn't believe in. This view made his heart hard. Ultimately, he landed in the VA hospital to recover from the effects of the war.

"Man, they sent me a letter saying 'your friends and neighbors have asked that you serve your country.' I wanted to go to visit all of my neighbors to ask if they had called Uncle Sam and volunteered my services. It was total bullshit, Calvin. My neighbors didn't have anything to do with it. The Man was behind the whole thing."

I smiled. It tickled me to hear white men talk about "the Man." But Ken had been through something that literally terrified me. He could say anything he wanted.

"Lots of brothers over there, Calvin. They didn't like honkies, but we were cool, me and the brothers. We looked out for each other. We all had to hang together, because Charlie was a bitch. Man, it would rain for days. We'd be soaking wet and cold. We froze our asses off."

It seemed as though he had hundreds of stories about the war. He called it being "in country." Vietnam sounded like a horrible place filled with gooks, jungle foliage, and pot-smoking American soldiers.

"I saw my buddies get shot up over there. It was scary. Guys were getting arms and legs blown off and screaming. I was even scared to take a piss. I didn't want to get shot with my pants down, you know. You had to be careful lighting a cigarette at night, because you could get shot from a mile away. But you know what the scariest shit was? Going out on patrol and looking for 'VC.'"

"What's that?"

"That's when some of us would go out ahead of the platoon to check things out. There'd be several of us. We'd spread out and form a triangle. The guy up front would be on point and he would lead the way with the other two guys on his flanks. There were land mines and booby traps. You couldn't see a damn thing because of the thick jungle, you know."

Now my friends and neighbors had concocted a scheme for me, just as they had done for Ken. Uncle Sam needed my service, so had he sent me to Southeast Asia too.

My hospital room walls were all glass. Beyond them, I could see the thick, green, moist jungle foliage surrounding the confines of my room. Suddenly, something rustled in the thick green leaves! I sat up in my bed, on full alert.

I stood out here, all alone on the point. My buddies had fallen back, so I leaped out of the bed and grabbed my M-16 from the corner of the room. More rustling.

Dammit, show yourself!

A faceless figure dressed in green fatigues, wearing a pointed straw hat, darted by the room in a fleeting moment and disappeared in the brush as quickly as he had appeared. I ducked behind the bed for cover. When the coast cleared, I got back in the bed but kept my eyes trained on the windows.

The Viet Cong kept running by my room, hour after hour and day after day. They never saw me, even though I lay in the open on my bed. Even though they never saw me, I ducked every time one of them ran by. They seemed to be in hasty retreat from someone or something. I heard bullets whizzing by, but no one ever got hit.

Chapter 11

THE ROUNDTABLE

Prayers Go Up and the Doctors Solve a Mystery

DOC MADE IT TO HOUSTON A few days after I'd been admitted to St. Luke's. My sister Linda had come with her. I had no idea they had arrived because I busily dodged Viet Cong and paid little attention to anything else going on around me. After they got a room at a hotel in the Medical Center, Doc's sole mission became finding out what went wrong with her beloved CK.

"What happened to you, CK?"

I stared at her with a glassy look and tried desperately to focus over the oxygen mask covering my nose and mouth. My voice bordered on inaudibility as I mustered all my might to whisper. "I had a cold, and the kids brought me here."

I never said a word to Linda or even looked at her. She left the room and began to emit a deep gut-wrenching wail. I had been *her* best friend for forty years. The fact that I didn't address her broke her heart. I didn't mean any harm, but I didn't acknowledge any strangers. After a short while, she left the hospital and returned to the hotel room. Seeing me lying virtually motionless and out of it upset her to the core of her soul.

Rod's birthday had come and gone. I hadn't died as the doctors had expected, but I wasn't out of the woods. The Stallion's heart kept beating even though x-rays of his lungs displayed cloudy infection. The strong antibiotic cocktail didn't do its job. The high fever would not subside. Dr. Tran couldn't tell Doc anything. My speech got progressively quieter and slurred with each passing day. Virtually no one except Rod understood what I whispered. I could barely move my arms and legs. My motor skills had badly deteriorated.

That night, the Colts played a preseason game in Mexico City against the Pittsburgh Steelers. Rod and I never missed a home game, even after I moved to Houston, because I had flown to Indy to catch the Falcons game a couple weeks earlier. If the Colts played away from Indianapolis's RCA Dome, we'd watch the game at our respective homes and call each other throughout the contest.

"Man, did you see that? What a horrible call!"

Rod later told me, I watched the game with him and seemed to be attentive. I couldn't remember anything about it at all by the time he left the next day.

I also didn't recall my sister Linda earned a living as a hairdresser. She nosily explored my apartment to learn what her big brother had going on in Houston. She found a well-kept flat, nicely appointed and decorated. During her search, she stumbled across my hair clippers. Since my lifelong barber, Mr. Files, lived 1,200 miles away, I cut my own hair. Linda brought the clippers to the hospital to practice her trade. Surely this loving gesture would jolt my memories of her. She had me propped up so she could give me a haircut and shave before Rod left to go home the next day. Regrettably, this tender and meticulous grooming didn't help. I still couldn't remember her.

Rod tried to help jumpstart my memory. "This is Linda. She is your sister, Calvin."

"Cashflow, you don't remember me?" She used my "line" name given to me when I pledged into the Alpha Phi Alpha fraternity many years before. It had become a term of endearment that only my mom, brother, and sisters used. It didn't work. I stared blankly has she removed the oxygen mask to lovingly give me a haircut and shave.

Through the years, Linda had been a person of great faith. She owned a gentle and kind spirit, and she had a heart for the downtrodden. The contempt I felt for her when we were young kids had long since disappeared. Linda had become my kind friend. We shared an apartment before I got married. Unlike some siblings who don't get along, the four of us loved each other more and more as the years passed. Even though my baby sister Carla wasn't in Houston, she knew every detail about my condition from Doc.

Linda listened carefully to what the doctors were saying. After one conference, one of the young doctors who worked with Dr. Kielhofner turned to Linda.

"We don't know what's wrong yet. We're just going to pray for him."

Linda didn't need to hear anything else. "I'm not worried anymore," she told Doc. A miracle had been birthed.

The doctors weren't the only ones praying, and Linda wasn't the only person of faith around me. It sounds like a cliché, but when I couldn't pray for myself, others leaped into action to do it for me. My mother prayed. Her friends prayed. My co-workers prayed. Bernice and the kids prayed. People I didn't even know prayed for my recovery. My family had gotten the word out that I needed God's help.

The Bible is replete with scriptures that speak to the power of prayer in our lives. When God's people agree in prayer, He moves. God had made promises to me. The promises were of peace, prosperity, abundance of life, and healing. Over the years I had hidden those promises in my heart. My life roles were not only limited to Doc's golden child and a person of "firsts." I belonged to God. I enjoyed being his child. I understood my role as one of his favorites and most beloved. He heard the cries of his children about me. Yes, I had been stubborn and made some mistakes in my life, but he still loved me more than anyone else ever could. He had a plan for my life. Someone would be blessed, helped and strengthened by my experience with all of this. Prayers had gone up, so now the time had come for things to start falling in place for delivery of the miracle.

The testing had continued, and some of the results had come in. Dr. Kielhofner and her partner from Houston Infectious Diseases Associates, along with a roundtable of other doctors, had made a startling discovery. It had been a little over a week since I had been admitted to St. Luke's. What the doctor's roundtable concluded is that I had tested positive for *Legionella*, the bacteria that causes Legionnaire's disease.

Like the people who attended the Legionnaire's convention in 1976, I had all the classic symptoms of Legionnaire's disease, including pneumonia, headache, fever, diarrhea, cough, shortness of breath, and confusion. I had become one of the 10,000–18,000 Americans who contract this awful disease each year. By law, the hospital had to report my case to the Center for Disease Control. An investigation ensued to determine where I contracted the bacteria.

Many people remember the terrible outbreak of the disease in Philadelphia in 1976. There had been other mass outbreaks since then. Notwithstanding the highly publicized mass outbreaks, most cases of Legionnaire's disease occur sporadically. That's exactly what had happened to me as there had been no reports of an outbreak at the hotel I stayed at in Chicago a few days earlier. In addition, no evidence of the bacteria presented itself in my apartment complex, call center building, or main campus of the corporation where I worked. In a bizarre twist, my colleague Brenda also came down with pneumonia a week after I got sick. Fortunately, she didn't have Legionnaire's disease.

It really didn't matter where I contracted the Legionnaire's bacteria. There were additional long-term consequences for me to deal with. In very rare instances, Legionnaire's disease is accompanied by dysfunction of the cerebellum, the part of the brain that controls muscle coordination.

Years later, Dr. Tiwari, Dr. Kielhofner, and one of their colleagues, Dr. Samuel Shelburne, would write a case study about dysfunction of the cerebellum with Legionnaire's. Their paper, titled "Cerebellar Involvement in Legionellosis," published in the *Southern Medical Journal* in February 2004, disclosed that they found only twenty-nine cases where this happened. I belonged to this small population of people with this rare complication, and it would change my life forever. As a result I developed a condition known as dysarthria.

The condition is a motor speech disorder. The muscles of the mouth, face, and respiratory system become weak, move slowly, or don't move at all after a stroke or other brain injury. The type and severity of dysarthria depend on which area of the nervous system is affected. A person with dysarthria may experience any of the following symptoms, depending on the extent and location of damage to the nervous system:

- "Slurred" speech
- Speaking softly or barely able to whisper
- Slow rate of speech
- Limited tongue, lip, and jaw movement
- Abnormal intonation (rhythm) when speaking
- Changes in vocal quality
- Hoarseness
- Breathiness
- Drooling or poor control of saliva
- Chewing and swallowing difficulty

Five or six days after being admitted to St. Luke's, I began to experience every one of these symptoms. My lifelong ability to sing, talk, yell, whistle, and every other function related to speech, vanished in a matter of days. Even something as simple as chewing gum would prove to be impossible for me. I would never again sing in a choir, lead worship, conduct meetings at work, give presentations, or cheer at a Colts game.

More bad news came. Something caused the dysarthria. The culprit was another condition called ataxia. Ataxia usually is a result of damage to the cerebellum from disease, infection, or injury. It can develop over time or come on suddenly, depending on the cause. Signs and symptoms of ataxia include:

- Unsteady walk
- Tendency to stumble
- Slurred speech
- Difficulty with fine-motor tasks, such as eating or buttoning a shirt

- Slow eye movements
- Difficulty swallowing

This explained my problems with moving my limbs and speaking. Working out with Michele or Team Fudd, teasing my buddies during a run, or even working out alone would be in question going forward.

Chapter 12
NEVER BETTER

A Short but Powerful Anecdote

THREE DAYS AFTER THE DOCTORS DISCOVERED the diagnosis of Legionnaire's disease, Linda and Doc prepared to leave Houston to return to Indiana. With each passing hour, I became more and more lucid and finally remembered Linda. I remembered Carla too. I did have sisters after all! There were no more trips to the tunnel, bakery, or Vietnam for me. My family had come to my rescue. I realized I had nearly died from Legionnaire's disease, but thanks to the grace and healing power of God, and the expertise of gifted doctors, I lived. I had received the best care possible for my condition.

I felt overwhelmingly tired. All I wanted to do was sleep. Every couple of hours, around the clock, nurses came to draw blood from my arms, so although I felt exhausted, sleep didn't come easily. At first, the needles felt like spears. They plunged into my forearms with force and velocity. My arms had gotten alarmingly thin after two weeks in the hospital with no solid food. The needles looked as thick as my forearms.

I wondered how heroin addicts could endure giving themselves shots. Maybe they got used to the stinging digs under their skin. I did. After a couple days of being awakened constantly, for round after round of getting speared for blood, I got used to it. I didn't even wince after a while. I started to look forward to it as a personal challenge to endure pain and would maintain a hollow stare with every puncture. On top of these jabs, IVs had become a permanent appendage to my hands, which were bruised from multiple injections.

The doctors ordered a fresh battery of tests. They evaluated my brain and chest carefully with various scans. All the results were within normal limits. They switched the medicine to treat the *legionella* to more powerful antibiotics and gave me steroids for treatment of my central nervous system. Of course, The Stallion's heart kept beating, and all of the other non-pulmonary functions, such as my renal and liver functions, were fine. Nevertheless, I had a long road ahead.

How I contracted Legionnaire's remained a mystery. I had survived, but the disease really messed me up. I could barely move. When I tried to talk, no one could understand me. The high fever had taken its toll. Prepping for a CT scan provided an indicator of how far I had to go. In order to complete the test, I simply had to drink a cup of cranberry-flavored fluid that would serve as a contrast. There were two glaring problems. First, I hated cranberry juice with a passion, and second, I no longer swallowed normally.

Unfortunately, no one knew I would have problems with this. As I prepared for the scan, the attendant helped me sit up and tried to help me drink the contrast. The gagging began immediately. The thought of downing cranberry juice grossed me out completely. I couldn't swallow the liquid that did make its way to my throat. I coughed, spit up, and choked violently. Try as I might, I could not get the contrast fluid down. The result was another IV to inject the contrast into my body.

Even though my body had been ravaged, my mind started to flex its muscles. As the fog in my mind slowly burned off, my thoughts started to string together. There were no more rooms misted in flour or walled with jungle foliage. There were only thoughts about my current predicament. How fast would the medicine help me get back on my feet and back to work?

My mind fell on my colleague, Glenn. Tears welled in my eyes has I thought about him. He took the ill-fated trip to Chicago with me. Was he okay? I tried to ask, but the words wouldn't come out. He had quietly but solidly supported me from day one. I would be devastated if something happened to him. I had to know.

"Is….G….G…Gl….enn…o…kay?" I couldn't believe how much effort it took getting that simple question out.

Glenn had returned to work after our trip to Chicago with no ill effects at all. The news lifted a gargantuan weight of my mind. He wouldn't have to go through what I had to overcome. I was responsible for him; after all, I had been the one to pursue the idea of making the trip to Chicago. Even though the kind and caring staff at St. Luke's made me as comfortable as they could, the guilt associated with Glenn contracting Legionnaire's disease, and enduring life in intensive care, would have been unbearable for me.

The evidence of that caring manifested itself when the time came for an MRI. The test could be frightening for someone with claustrophobia. I had just overcome being bound and held captive. The thought of tight spaces or close confines scared me to death. MRIs are conducted inside a huge buzzing machine that looks like something from Star Wars. The patient receiving the MRI is strapped down to a narrow cot built into the huge device. The cot slides all the way into a tube containing electronics that facilitate the capture of a high-definition, panoramic image of the subject body part. In my case, the target was my head. During the process, the patient hears a series of loud knocking sounds, similar to a mini jack hammer, while they are strapped down and required to lay motionless inside the imaging tube. The examination could last for upward of forty-five minutes.

The attendant strapped my head into place. Immediately, the images of chocking and gagging during the last test and being bound in the bakery came rushing back to mind. A look of terror covered my face. The aide saw my face and gently and carefully explained the process. I would slide into the tube so that an image of my head could be produced. He asked me to be as still as I could.

"Try to relax, Mr. King. We're going to do a series of pictures of your head. I need you to be still." He put his hand on my shoulder. "This won't hurt you. I promise."

I thought, *No problem, dude. I can barely move anyway.* I just nodded. As the ride into the tube began, I closed my eyes.

"This process doesn't hurt at all. Don't worry. Just think of something pleasant, but don't move. Remember—try to think of something pleasant."

So I did. The ride into the tube reminded me of other rides.

Nearly every Sunday morning, between 5:30 and 6:00 am, I donned riding gear, cleats, and my helmet. I mounted my Cannondale bike to embark on a fifty-mile ride into the Texas countryside. During March, April, and May, the early morning temperatures were in the low to mid sixty-degree range. Most times, little humidity accompanied a brilliant sunrise. All these elements made for postcard picture-perfect mornings in the Houston area. These were delightful conditions for a long bike ride to get way from everything.

I would pedal out of my apartment complex to head for the outskirts of town. About eleven miles into the ride, I would cross the Sam Houston Tollway and move steadily south of the city. From that point, the buildings slowly give way to thick green pastures dotted by beautiful bluebonnets in the Texas countryside.

Once I cycled past the small hamlets of Fresno and Arcola, I would be all alone on a two-lane highway with wide shoulders for safe riding in the country. On those mornings, I rode near farms, ranches, and under the blue sky. I would wave at cows and marvel at the beauty of the bluebonnets. Occasionally, I would see other cyclists and we would exchange a salute as we passed. These morning rides yielded a totally wonderful rejuvenation.

One Sunday morning as I rode my familiar route, I had an unusual welcoming committee about twenty-five miles into the ride. As I sped down the shoulder of the road at twenty miles per hour, I saw large objects up ahead to my right, perched on top of the fence separating the pasture and the road. Usually on bike rides in the country, I kept a watchful eye for dogs. Some of them love to chase cyclists. Dogs never sit on top of fences, so something else loomed ahead. As I pedaled closer, I realized these images were very large birds. There were five of them: huge turkey buzzards waiting for carcasses. These were the biggest birds I had ever seen in my entire life. Their eyes followed me as I zoomed by, as if they willed me to take a bad spill and end up a bloody, mangled tasty breakfast.

"Sorry, boys. There's no meal for you here." My heart rate leaped to a crescendo as I waved at them while nervously picking up the pace to get away as quickly as I could. I had never seen buzzards up close, so I wasn't sure if they would fly toward me or not. I didn't stick around to find out. They were still there as I passed them on the return trip back into town. Afterward, every time I thought of seeing buzzards lined up on a fence waiting for a meal, I laughed.

I smiled to myself, while inserted into the small MRI tube, strapped to a cot, and surrounded by the knocking and jack hammering. I was on my bike, healthy and strong, in the Texas countryside on cool crisp Sunday morning. The cows, horses, bluebonnets, and buzzards waved at me as I zipped by without a care in the world.

Every day my intensive care nurse, Sonia, would start the day the same way.

"What day is it today, Mr. King?"

She helped me cheat. She had written the date on the whiteboard in my room. I turned my head and stared at the board. It was August 25. I had been in the hospital thirteen days. I was stunned. Why couldn't I remember any of this?

"Au...gust...twen...ty... fifth." It took everything within me, every ounce of strength, to slur the date one syllable at a time, my voice barely eked out above a whisper. Drool ran down my chin. It was my new method of speaking.

"That's right. It's a wonderful day!" She repeated this ritual every day, until I left intensive care.

Sonia was an angel. She wiped drool from my chin, moved me around, and made me comfortable. Someone had brought in a picture of me running the Indianapolis Marathon from a couple years back. I looked powerful and fit in the photograph which demanded attention.

"Who is that guy in the picture? Is that you? *Wow!*"

In fact, every one of the staff members and doctors who came in made a comment about the picture. They probably couldn't believe the half-dead guy lying in the intensive care room all wired up with a face covered by an oxygen mask was the same guy in the picture. It was an incredible contrast.

At home, a 24 x 36 inch poster of the same picture hung in my living room. I placed it there to remind myself of my running prowess. It inspired me at home before workouts, and now, it showed others the real Cal; a strong and determined warrior.

Even though Sonia's kindness comforted him, the warrior didn't want his mama to leave his bedside. I understood even though I wanted her there, she had to get back to work. Up until my odyssey, Doc's sixty-one-year-old eyes were focused on retiring from her job at Fort Wayne State Hospital. The facility housed mentally impaired individuals. She had cared for mentally challenged people for nearly thirty years. Many of those years, she had been working to support herself. The work ethic Price Love taught her fifty years ago still formed an imprint on her brain. She knew how to care for people who had brain damage or other crippling disabilities. Her years of work in this field taught her the temperament to minister to these folks.

Now, her golden child received the benefit of her caring spirit. When almost everyone around me was weepy and concerned, mom exuded strength and confidence. She never wavered in her faith that God would help the doctors caring for me figure out what was going on. I would be healed. In many ways, I believe she single-handedly willed me from the brink of death. She told everyone the same thing, "God's going to raise him!"

Before they left for Indiana, Linda whispered in my ear, "Stop being mean to Bernice. Let her stay here." Doc, Linda, and Rod had all seen me treat Bernice coolly, even when I was totally out of it. I had repeatedly asked her to go home. I'd also been telling my family to make her leave. They wouldn't. It had made them uncomfortable and unsure how to handle the situation.

"Calvin, she doesn't work, so she can stay here to look after you until you get on your feet. We gotta go home to work. Somebody has to take care of you." To her credit, Bernice had been nothing but kind. She had the compassion of Christ. She did manage a successful business with Mary Kay Cosmetics, so she had responsibilities too. It had to be embarrassing for her that I asked her to leave or told my family members to tell her to leave almost every day. I really couldn't make anyone do anything in my condition. All I could do was comply with my family's wishes and make the best of it.

With that, Doc was gone; however, she remained confident I would recover. She thanked all her friends for praying for me when she went to church the following Sunday. They continued a prayer and fasting regimen. One encounter got her blood boiling.

Dr. Towles had been my personal doctor (and a longtime friend of my mom and dad for many, many years), until he quit his private practice to take a position as a corporate physician. His skill as a surgeon gained him notoriety, making him a larger-than-life man. I admired his strong handshake and warm, gentle voice. Most of all, Dr. Towles gained respect in our community for his knowledge, integrity, and professionalism. He attended Union Baptist Church, the oldest and most prestigious black Baptist Church in Fort Wayne. Doc also held a membership there. She had gotten the word out to the pastor and parishioners concerning my condition and diagnosis in Houston. They were all pulling for me, especially the pastor, Reverend Hunter, my friend and fraternity brother.

I really hadn't seen Dr. Towles in quite some time. However, when the news of my contracting Legionnaire's disease reached him, in his opinion, I wouldn't survive. His mistake was sharing that opinion with Doc after a church service.

"You know, people don't recover from that disease, sister King."

"I don't receive that at all! My son will recover fully. Dr. Towles, you should be ashamed of yourself. You know God is able to heal my son. He's going to heal him." With that she turned and walked away.

Dr. Towles wasn't being mean spirited or showing a lack of faith. He simply shared his honest and professional opinion. Generally, this opinion rang true. If not treated, Legionnaire's claimed its victims more times than not. In my case, a miracle had been unleashed. Had not Kristi and Geoffrey come to visit when they did, I may have died alone in my apartment. It wasn't my time yet. I still had a long road ahead. My hard drive suffered severe burns, but my brain would simply have to find a way to rewire itself.

The healing began with the tremendous outpouring of care from friends. There were so many plants and flowers sent to the hospital, many of them had to be taken to my apartment. The volume simply crowded out the intensive care room. The president of my company, John Graf, and his wife sent the most beautiful flower arrangement I had ever seen. In addition to the flowers, literally hundreds of e-mails and cards were sent to the hospital with well wishes and kind thoughts. It made me think about work. I had to get better so I could get back into the groove of my career.

I had Legionnaire's disease. It sank in. Would I ever work again? I could barely move. No one could understand me. Kathleen still needed me, but I wasn't sure I would recover enough to handle things the same way I used to. Then I remembered something she told me when we were discussing her supervisor a couple of months before. The memory kindled a fire in me.

She told me that her boss, Carl, the guy who interviewed me six months before, would say the same thing to her every morning. He was one of the smartest people I had ever met. He commanded respect when he walked into a room, but he was totally down-to-earth. He made all of us better. As Kathleen told me many times, he was demanding yet fair. It was all true.

When she told me the simple two-line story, I just laughed and didn't give it much thought. Now the story had a whole new meaning for me altogether. The dialogue of this simple story was amazingly short:

Kathleen: "Hey, good morning, Carl, how you doing?"

Carl: "Great, Kathleen, never better!"

"Cal, he always says the same thing every morning."

"Really? Every day?"

"Yep. Every day."

Day after day after day after day, the response never changed.

"Never better."

Rain, sunshine, hot, windy, calm, cold; it didn't matter. The answer was always the same.

I kept thinking about that story as I lay in intensive care trying to recover. What would make a person say they were never better every single day? So many people secretly battle depression, illness, and loneliness. Still others battle addiction, abusive relationships, and problem children. I'd seen people worry about excessive debt, missed deadlines, and disabilities. Now I had Legionnaire's disease and the stigma that would go along with that. The solution had to be perseverance. Perseverance gives us the ability to go through troubles and trials of all kinds. Perseverance makes sure we don't give up while experiencing the inevitable troubles of life. I believed there had to be more.

Over the years, one of my favorite books of the Bible had been Lamentations. There is a passage in the third chapter I read many times:

"I remember my affliction and my wandering, the bitterness and the gall. I well remember them, and my soul is downcast within me. Yet this I call to mind and therefore I have hope. Because of the Lord's great love we are not consumed, for his compassions never fail. They are new every morning; great is your faithfulness." (Lamentations 3:19–23 NIV)

The King James translation of this scripture says God's *mercies* are new every morning. I had solved the riddle of why Carl answered "never better" each day. It had to be a combination of his perseverance, hope, and God's great love and mercy. They all work together to keep us from being consumed. This has to be an everyday thing. God's compassion rests upon us every morning and we have to firmly believe that this day will be an outstanding day. We have to have hope and believe we can overcome any adversity in our lives every single day, through God's mercy, grace, and our sheer determination.

If I could run marathons, I could overcome this. If I could get picked out of a crowd and given a shot at working on a great career, I could overcome this. I started to think about all the great things that had happened during my lifetime. Doc was right. God would raise me up. My resurrection represented a personal Y2K remediation.

A suite of new life lessons awaited me. These wouldn't come from Doc or Pops. They would spawn from this dark place called Legionnaire's disease, the event life's discontinuity presented to me. They would be the new guiding principles of my life. My dear friend, Tom, has the Yoder rules of life; now I could start my own. The first new rule of life for me: Each day is a wonderful day.

Doesn't matter if the sun isn't shining or there's ten inches of snow on the ground and the wind chill factor is minus ten degrees. It doesn't matter how people treat me, how I feel, whether I'm rich or poor, black, white, or high yellow. I'm alive, and therefore, it's a wonderful day.

I wanted Carl to come see me so I could tell him I had solved the mystery. He promised to visit me a couple days after he learned I'd asked for him. His promise humbled me. What a huge deal. The senior executive vice president of my company had committed time to see me. The morning of his visit, I remained in intensive care, but the oxygen mask and the monitors were gone. Sonia had gotten me dressed and sat me up to receive Carl.

"Hey, Cal! How's it going?"

My eyes lit up when I saw Carl. He walked over to me and shook my hand. He was one of my heroes. I tried to say "never better," but when I opened my mouth the words wouldn't come out clearly. They were a garbled mess. I drooled onto my pajama shirt when I tried to speak. All I could do was smile and nod. Carl knew I was glad to see him. He wore a gracious smile.

Some people may have been embarrassed about drooling in front of such an important man. Last time I had had a one-on-one exchange with him, I wore a gray pin-striped suit, a crisp white shirt, spit-shined shoes, and a handsome tie. I spoke with affable and silver-tongued tones. I sipped orange juice and exchanged pleasantries. I explained why I believed Fed Ex had burst on the scene and competed with—and won against—UPS. The discontinuity theory explained the phenomenon. We talked for almost an hour. Today, I had on PJs, drooled, smiled, and nodded as Carl did all the talking. I was never better.

His graciousness filled my small hospital room, and he didn't rush his visit. The conversation wasn't deep or profound, but it meant the world to me. Later, he would share the details of his visit with Kathleen. Carl had an insight he shared with her. "A lot of things have to go just right for us to function every day."

Psalms 139:14 (NIV) says, "I praise you because I am fearfully and wonderfully made; your works are wonderful, I know that full well."

The passage supports what Carl said. It emphasizes the incredible nature of our physical bodies. The human body is the most complex and unique organism in the world, with complexity and uniqueness personally designed by God. My body had been altered, but I was never better, because I lived.

Chapter 13

FLEXING MUSCLES

Trying to Conquer Physical Challenges

AFTER CARL'S VISIT, I CLEARLY KNEW communicating with visitors and friends would be difficult if not nearly impossible. I just couldn't bring myself to settle for that fate. My mind continued to sharpen with each passing day. It slowly returned to a semblance of its quick wit and mental dexterity. Except for periods of short-term memory loss, my mind began to move lucidly from topic to topic. Even though I would hide the lapses, it would be a challenge that would persist for years. Otherwise, my mind moved at light speed, while my mouth moved at about five miles an hour. I could spit out a few syllables every hour, even though those syllables weren't clear to anyone but me.

I thought hard about how to overcome this temporary communication obstacle. My fingers were now working well enough that I could move them and even grip a pen or pencil. I scribbled notes, but they were just that, a bunch of scribbling. My writing required uninterrupted concentration and time. Even then, those reading it found it barely legible.

I discovered there are simple tasks "normal" people take for granted every day. Talking, moving limbs and writing are just few. I felt another rule of life coming on:

Never take the simple things for granted.

Carl had it right. A lot of things have to go right for us to function every day. I decided since I could move my fingers, I could hunt and peck letters on a keyboard to share my thoughts with others. The idea came from a movie I saw once in which a hearing-impaired man had a special phone called a Telecommunication Device for the Deaf (TDD phone or TTY phone). This special phone allowed him to type words in order to carry on a conversation. Surely, I could communicate with visitors via typing words on a laptop.

Someone called Glenn to share this solution to my communication challenge. Shortly thereafter, he appeared in my room with a shiny new laptop computer. His winning smile filled the room as he carefully walked me through the log-in process. Typing letters proved more difficult than I ever imagined. It required a dexterity level my fingers refused to attain. Maybe this wouldn't be my new method of communication after all. The natural sending of and receiving messages via speech happens quickly. I simply couldn't type quickly enough to simulate vocal exchanges.

Visiting with Glenn stirred other emotions besides the natural joy of seeing a true friend and colleague. Deep inside, my mind's questions simmered to a full boil. I couldn't help but ask God these questions even though my parents had raised me never to question God. I reasoned I wouldn't know the answers if I didn't ask.

Why did this happen to me but not Glenn? After all, we had taken the same trip, ate at the same restaurants, and stayed at the same hotel. It just wasn't fair. The heaviness of guilt pushed me down as these questions began to ring louder and louder in my head. Glenn had been my friend. I shouldn't be jealous of his health or disappointed that I fought the fight against Legionnaire's disease alone. Even though I slowly began to recover, this whole scenario confused me.

Asking questions served me well as I climbed the corporate ladder. I had a favorite question for those around me presenting projects or sharing ideas in meetings:

"Why?"

My life wasn't a corporate merger or strategic plan. There were no easy answers. I could do nothing more than simply persevere and let the answer to these questions play out over time.

Day by day, it became somewhat easier to move my extremities. The only difference I noticed was my arms and legs wouldn't move without me concentrating and commanding them to move. People take involuntary limb movement for granted. I didn't have that luxury. I'd look at my leg and say *move* in order for anything to happen. This taxed and left me exhausted. However, the good news continued for me. By the last week in August, I could sit up by myself. I could move my legs, but I hadn't been out of the bed for days. The time had come to master walking.

My pulse quickened, and my eyes danced around the room. I hadn't walked in three weeks. The excitement waned quickly. After a couple steps, every muscle in my legs screamed in agony and punished me with vicious cramps for making them endure inactivity. My hamstring and calf muscles knotted up like rope. The pain was more severe than any charley horse I ever had from track practice or running marathons. Sonia helped me back into bed after just a few horrible steps. I decided I didn't want to walk anymore. Of course, that wasn't acceptable. I got a comforting massage to ease the cramping.

Wheelchairs work wonders for people who can't walk under their own power. I used to pay little attention or care to those confined to wheelchairs. That all changed when I took a ride from my room to the front entryway of St. Luke's. Even though everyone seemed very tall as I rolled by, it was a huge step to finally make it outside into the late August sun. Thank goodness for wheelchairs.

I squinted to shield my eyes from the bright summer sun. I'd forgotten about the intense heat and humidity of Houston. Who cared? I was alive. The hot summer sun charged me up. I knew soon, trips outside to my neighborhood would be on my terms. St. Luke's is literally only three or four city blocks from Rice University were I had logged hundreds of miles running and biking. I filled my lungs with a huge gulp of sun-drenched air. With closed eyes and the heat dancing on my head, thoughts about pedaling the Black Beauty in the Texas countryside on a trip to see the cows, horses, buzzards, and bluebonnets filled my mind and my heart. I kicked my feet and smiled to myself.

The next day produced another big step. I graduated from the intensive care unit to St. Luke's rehab hospital. With this move came a change in the doctor responsible for my care. This is where I would meet "Dr. K," of Texas Medical Center Rehab, the man who would, in part, hold the key to my future.

All the nurses helping me through physical therapy talked to me about meeting Dr. K. They had a healthy respect for him. He ordered a comprehensive physical therapy program designed to help me improve my eye-hand coordination, motor skills, and ambulatory functions.

The rehab hospital was heaven. No more monitors, no more IVs, but best of all, no more waking up every two hours during the night to give blood. I didn't have any left anyway, because I had become a victim of vampires. The intensive care staff had taken virtually all of my blood. Even though nurses assigned to me weren't waking me up every two hours, my body had gotten used to the regimen played out in intensive care. Consequently, it took a couple days for me to sleep through the night. I felt the chronic fatigue that resulted from Legionnaire's disease and sleeplessness.

The food tasted better in rehab. The only qualm I had about the food was its soft consistency. Because I couldn't swallow worth a darn, each meal arrived pureed. I wanted a cheese burger in the worst way, but solid food or liquid made me choke if I wasn't extremely careful. An ultrasound test showed that instead of swallowing in one motion, the things I ingested would start to flow, stop, pool, and then continue down my throat in a two-step process. For some reason, drinking through a straw helped solve this condition. This change in the way I swallowed would persist for years.

Days were planned with various physical therapy activities. This involved short trips to a room with apparatuses designed to help people gain dexterity and movement. People like me, who had suffered some type of illness or injury that robbed them of the movements we all take for granted, were scattered throughout the room. There were stroke victims, automobile accident survivors, and people recovering from all sorts of maladies affecting ambulatory skill. Each day, I looked around and saw people worse off than me. Although I had become a physical mess, I found myself thankful to be as well as I was. This bolstered my resolve to conquer each and every exercise, including walking and riding a stationary bike.

Walking the floor became my favorite physical therapy exercise. My hamstrings and calves weren't angry at me anymore. I learned to walk again, without fear of the crippling cramps that greeted me when I first tried to take steps in intensive care. Although I could walk again, I couldn't quite manage the course on my own. The ataxia had affected my natural gait. So to get me through the exercise, the physical therapists tied a band around my waist to control the walk and help keep me from falling.

The pace picked up every day. The goal of physical therapy centered on getting me comfortable with walking again. My goal exceeded the staff's goal by a wide margin. This comeback would show my road racing capabilities. I tried to go as fast as I could each day. *Memorial Park, here I come,* was the battle cry in my head.

As much as I enjoyed the thrill of each walking session, they would leave me totally spent. All I'd want to do when I got back to the room was take a nap. I didn't complain, because being on my feet again made me more than thankful. Doc had been right all along. I wasn't running five-minute miles, but God had raised me.

While the movement thing went well, the speech therapy didn't. My speech therapist, Sarah, tried to determine what I could do. Sarah looked much too young to teach me anything. She didn't look any older than my daughter, Kristi. Sarah tried to get me to sound out letters in the same manner as preschool children are taught.

"Okay, Mr. King, repeat after me...pa, pa, pa, pa...la, la, la."

"Pa...pa...la...la...la." My tongue didn't want to move, and I couldn't stop drooling.

"Okay, now click your tongue like this, cluck, cluck, cluck..." Sarah performed the simple sound made as a result of clicking her tongue off the roof of her mouth.

I tried, and I tried, and I tried, but I couldn't do it at all!

"It's okay. You can rest now. Just keep practicing." She clicked her tongue off the roof her mouth and smiled at me.

When she left, I cried like a baby. I just couldn't believe how hard it was to perform this simple movement of my tongue. Kids click their tongues all the time, yet I found it impossible for me to do it. After my pity party ended, I tried clicking again and again. It was no use. I'd have to keep working on this.

Before I left the rehab hospital, my friends, Jim and Laura—who had also left Lincoln Life to follow Kathleen to Houston—got permission to visit me. They chatted with me for an hour. They talked while I nodded, drooled, and tried a few syllables, none of which were very clear. The conversation had wandered all over the place including a discussion about a mutual friend who happened to be gay. By that time, they were about to leave. I walked with them toward the exit of the hospital.

Jim made a reference to the mutual friend once more. Incredibly, intelligible words came out of my mouth.

"The gay boy?" I smiled.

Laura and Jim laughed and teased me. "We've been talking an hour, and that's the first thing you said we could understand, Cal."

My face got white hot. I didn't want them to think I had anything against gay people at all. I didn't. The statement simply affirmed I remembered who they were talking about. That was a big deal for me, because my memory had been spotty. The moment passed without an explanation on my part. I smiled and embraced them before they left. This farewell exchange made me sad. I couldn't keep up verbally or express my feelings, and I didn't want Jim and Laura to leave.

My mind fell on Michele. I missed her so much, and I wanted to tell her everything going on with me. I wondered when I would see her smile, smell her perfume, and hear her giggle again. She had called Lois several times to get updates on my condition because of the strict orders that everyone from work leave me alone. That order shouldn't have applied to her, but I couldn't change that.

I made my way back to the twenty-seventh floor of the hospital to rest. At least my muscles were working again, even if my mouth didn't.

Part III
RESILIENCE

Chapter 14

HOME AGAIN

Leaving the Hospital Behind

I COULD IMMEDIATELY SEE WHY THE staff loved Dr. George Kevorkian. He had a gentle and kind bedside manner. When I first heard his surname, my curiosity took over. I wondered if he was related to Jack Kevorkian, the alleged "suicide doctor" from Michigan who had been accused of assisting nearly one hundred people end their lives in the 1990s. I never learned the answer. It didn't matter. Their methods were polar opposites. Dr. K made sure I would be able to live well and function before he would release me to go home. After fully examining me, he warned me with a stern lecture to take it easy with eating.

"Mr. King, it would be a shame for you to have survived Legionnaire's disease and then choke to death." He made strong hand gestures for emphasis, and his face reflected the somber instructional tone. "You really, really have to be careful. Chew your food slowly. Take your time."

A month after nearly succumbing to Legionnaire's disease, I left St. Luke's hospital and rode to the comfortable flat in West U. Although I worried about my new limitations, a huge smile covered my face. Just as I did several months earlier as I rode from the airport to the hotel in Greenspoint, I rolled down the window on the passenger side of the car. I tried to enjoy all the warmth and sunshine I could during the short ride home.

Once I got home, I went straight to the bathroom. I wanted to take a long and measured look at myself. The huge mirror over the bathroom vanity, which had previously served as a stopover for one of the Brown Fellas, captured my reflection. It didn't show the picture of a six-foot, 180-pound, strong and muscular Stallion. The reflection showed a gaunt, middle-aged, light-skinned black man with hollow cheeks and sunken eyes peering through wire-rimmed glasses. I peeled off my clothes and stepped on the scale. I gasped in disbelief. All the finely chiseled muscles honed from years of running and biking were gone.

The needle moved ever so slowly. It stopped at 142 pounds! My limbs were skinny and my bones protruded. Except for my pale hue, I looked just like the images from Africa that tugged at people's hearts, compelling them to send donations.

I figured out very quickly that I couldn't take care of myself. I dropped utensils and glasses, lost my balance when walking through my apartment, and couldn't prepare meals for myself. Furthermore, eating or drinking resulted in violent choking. Worst of all, I had been sentenced to house arrest. The doctors wouldn't allow me to drive. I couldn't even walk to Kroger to go grocery shopping, though it was less than a hundred yards from my apartment. Linda had been right. I needed someone to take care of me, and they couldn't be there to do it.

So, over the next few weeks, Bernice stayed in Houston to help me. She prepared meals, talked to the doctors, worked with the insurance caseworker responsible for managing my treatment, and drove me to doctor visits and speech therapy. I felt like a complete and helpless invalid.

During a visit to Sarah, my speech therapist, it all caught up with me. I lost it. We had just worked through sounding out monosyllabic words and just a few polysyllabic words.

"Now, Mr. King, let's try to click your tongue again."

I still couldn't do it. How could I ever run a multimillion dollar call center when I couldn't even make a clucking sound? I had employees to inspire, tactical discussions to conduct with managers, prospects to impress, and staff meetings with Kathleen and the other directors. The thought of not being able to do those things anymore overwhelmed me. I sobbed a deep soul-wrenching cry, so loud everyone in the lobby could hear it. Bernice left the waiting room and came back to the office to see what was going on. I tried to tell them both what I felt, but I couldn't. I was a blubbering mess. She figured it out.

"He's upset because he can't talk, and he won't be able to do his job anymore."

When I heard that explanation, the wailing reached a crescendo. All they could do was try to comfort me. That was the first day I really questioned in earnest if I would ever work again. I had practiced speaking until I reached exhaustion, yet I couldn't string together sentences and no one could understand me.

It wasn't all doom and gloom for me. Kathleen called to say she wanted to visit. I couldn't speak the directions. I wrote them down on a pad and had them read to her over the phone. It took me a while to get it down, but I did. The printed note looked as though it had been written by an old man stricken with arthritis. Nevertheless, it served its purpose, because she got there at the appointed time.

"Hey, Cal, how's it going?"

"O—kay."

In my mind, I said *never better*. I was so happy to see her, because I felt as though her appearance reconnected me to my life. I hugged her as tight as I could as if doing so would free me from house arrest and send me speeding back to the life I had known before August 10. I don't think I had ever hugged her before. It felt a little awkward. Kathleen meant more to me than I think she understood. I respected her professionalism, but even more, I had been impressed with her intellect and passion to do things precisely. She was so bright, but yet she had an abundance of common sense. Many times, over the years, as I faced situations both professionally and personally, I found myself wondering how she would handle them. Now she symbolized the prize of self-determination, drive, and independence.

"What a neat picture. You look so powerful there."

She gazed at the huge poster of me, wearing navy blue running shorts and a white singlet, making my way through an Indianapolis park. The picture was taken as I competed in the Indianapolis Marathon. Now it prominently graced my living room wall. Although my memory failed from time to time, I remembered that day clearly. A secret story went along with the poster that showed me so strong and in complete control.

I had gone to Indianapolis in autumn 1998 to qualify for the Boston Marathon. Every serious marathoner wants to run Boston, but participating in it requires qualification. I remained the only member of Team Fudd who hadn't qualified, so they were all pulling for me. Yoder ran the race with me to help me qualify. The qualifying standard is age based. I needed to run the 26.2 miles in three hours and twenty minutes in order to make it. The race photographer captured the shot near mile sixteen, as I still ran smoothly under a 3:20 pace and looked like a strong physical specimen. Ultimately, my attempt at qualifying fell short again. I had previously tried three or four times without success.

By mile nineteen, I had started to cramp and bonked. I ended up finishing in well over three hours and missed my opportunity to go to Boston again. To add insult to injury, Tom qualified. Only the guys on Team Fudd knew that even though I looked great at that point, later my tongue would be hanging on the ground, and I would be one of many runners that day doing the death march from mile twenty to the finish. The casual observer of the poster would never hear the real story. Nevertheless, the poster served its purpose. It inspired me before workouts and impressed others. It impressed Kathleen that day.

"I brought something for you. It's the autobiography of Lance Armstrong, the Tour de France winner. You know, the cyclist?"

"Yep." I knew the Lance Armstrong story quite well.

"The story is really inspiring. It is all about Lance's life and surviving testicular cancer. His story reminded me of yours, Cal, so I thought you would enjoy this.

"Thank …you."

I did enjoy it. Legionnaire's disease hadn't robbed me of the love of reading. I pored over Lance's story. There were so many similarities in our stories, until I couldn't put the book down. He had been treated in the Houston Medical Center but ultimately decided to go to Indiana University Medical Center in Indianapolis for the most critical cancer treatment. Lance survived when the odds were stacked against him. He had decided to keep living his life. His iron will to survive and thrive was well documented. The title of the book said it all: *It's Not About the Bike: My Journey Back to Life.* If he could survive and get back to doing the things he loved, then so could I. Kathleen had hit a home run with this gift.

Lance's story inspired me, so I decided to go for my first "run." Bernice didn't think it was a good idea for me to go alone, so she laced up her sneakers to follow me. Nearly every morning before Legionnaire's, I had gone for runs in West U, either at Rice University or through the neighborhood near my apartment. I figured I'd go out the back of my complex, run a few blocks to Rice University. It should have been an easy run of no more than four miles round-trip. I'd leave Bernice far behind and conquer this thing on my own.

When I left St. Luke's, the doctors prescribed prednisone, a steroid that would help me get stronger and help with motor skills. One of the possible side effects of this steroid is a feeling of halo around the head. I envisioned the glass globe the cartoon characters on "The Jetsons" wore when they went into space. I had never experienced this side effect since leaving the hospital.

All that changed when I attempted my first run. The jogging lasted for two blocks. I stopped abruptly, gasping for air as I doubled over. Bernice just watched me.

"Are you okay?"

Someone had kicked all of the air out of my lungs. I couldn't say a word! I nodded as I bent over and rested my hands on my knees. After catching my breath, I decided to cross the street and start running toward Rice University again. I jogged a wobbly jog for about a block and had to stop. *Have I left Bernie?* Nope, she stood right behind me! I walked three more blocks. I had finished! With each step back to my place, the halo around me became more pronounced. By the time I walked into the apartment, it felt as though a fishbowl had been fitted firmly over my head. While I wasn't a world-class athlete, I knew firsthand how Lance must have felt on his maiden ride after surviving cancer.

A few days after my maiden run, I had a follow-up visit with Dr. Tiwari at her neighborhood clinic. This required a drive away from West U and the medical center. As we made our way to the clinic, a yellow school bus pulled next to us at a stop light. Of course I sat in the passenger seat with a clear view of the bus driver. This short, yellow bus probably transported special needs children. I'd been around people who made jokes about people who rode the "short bus." The jokes weren't funny anymore.

The next visit was to Dr. K to check my coordination and ambulatory ability. He thought I had progressed nicely and gave the approval for me fly to Indiana to continue convalescence. We scheduled a flight to Fort Wayne. I wasn't sure if I would ever be returning to Houston again except for follow-up visits with Dr. Tiwari. I wasn't even sure about that, because a neurologist in Fort Wayne had agreed to see me.

One thing was certain...I wanted to see Michele even though I knew it probably wouldn't happen. I had no way of seeing her, so I wrote an e-mail. I told her I missed her, and I hoped to see her again one day, to go for one of our rides around Houston, if I ever came back. The thought of never seeing her again brought tears to my eyes. Bernice read my e-mail to her. It made for a tense couple of days before the trip to Indiana. Although Michele would be blamed for spoiling our reconciliation, nothing was further from the truth. It simply wasn't Michele's doing—it was all mine.

While I didn't get to see Michele, I did get to see Lois. Lois was a native of the Houston area and had worked for our company over thirty years. She had always worked for the most senior executives in the office of the chairman. Although I had only known her for a few months, she had become very dear to me; my friend and confidant. She looked after me like an older sister would and was beloved by my family. Doc knew I loved Lois and asked about her nearly every time she called to check on me.

There were many days in which I charged hard without thinking about anything but making our call center the best in the industry. Lois kept a watchful eye on me. "Cal, you need to stop and eat lunch! Do you want me to get you something?" Her east Texas dialect had a calming effect.

On a bright sunny day at the end September, I got a ride to the call center to see my friend and Houston-based big sister. Lois met me in the parking lot. I wasn't there to see anyone else, and I didn't go into the building.

I stepped out of the car and walked to her. I could see the concern on her face when she saw my small frame. There was so much I wanted to tell her. I wanted to tell her about Randalls and Vietnam. I also wanted to tell her I was alright and that I'd be back as soon as I could.

None of those things were said. I could only manage two words:

"Hi, Lois."

We embraced. I knew she could feel my shoulder blades, but I didn't care. I felt perfectly safe with her. The next day, I would board a plane for Indiana. I didn't know if I would ever see Lois again. I cried softly as she embraced me.

Chapter 15
GOIN' BACK TO INDIANA

Returning to My Roots and a Second Opinion

ALL I'D EVER KNOWN WAS LIFE as a Hoosier. Although I had traveled extensively for work, I'd always returned to Fort Wayne. That's where my friends and family were. I had a sense that if I could go there for a while to gather myself, things would be okay. Besides, everyone wanted me to come back home. They all had their own personal stake and reasons. Bernice wanted to reconcile. Kristi and Geoff wanted their dad at home. Doc feared I could no longer care for myself, and my sisters thought their big brother "Cashflow" needed to be closer to home. I did miss Indiana. The paradox I would have to resolve was that I loved Houston, and I wanted to be there too. I had a job to do and I had begun a new life there. It was a big step for me to move to Houston and take an executive role. I wanted to see the project through on my terms. Unfortunately, I couldn't care for myself, and no one could stay in Houston with me.

October brought cooling temperatures to Indiana. The beautiful changing of the colors began as the majestic trees directed their green leaves to take on yellow, orange, brown, and red hues. The Hawk perched for a return, bringing with it the snow and cold. It meant harvest parties, high school football, and the most blessed day of the year—my birthday. There was much to look forward to. I had returned to get better. I spent most of October receiving visitors, taking naps, and going for walks. I tried to remember where I came from.

Sometimes, I would use my cell phone during afternoon walks to call Michele and other friends, but my garbled speech made those calls unproductive. I knew what I said, but most of the time the people on the other end of the phone didn't have a clue. My primary way of communication continued to be writing notes on pads. That just didn't work on a cell phone.

A couple Tri-Fudds came to see me a few days after I got home. Scott and Brian made me laugh heartily while they visited. Seeing them reminded me

111

of all the miles of running and cycling we had done over the years. I missed that camaraderie. As they were about to leave, Brian embraced me with tears streaming down his face. I didn't look well. He couldn't hide his fear that I might not finish this race.

"I…am…o…kay…Bri…an." I got that much out. Of course, a healthy dose of drool accompanied my affirmation. Even so, seeing Scott and Brian made me determined to run again.

Doc came to see me shortly after the Tri-Fudds left. She brought my favorite banana split ice cream. This particular visit seemed to rekindle an old spark of controversy.

"I brought CK some ice cream." Doc made what I thought was an innocent proclamation.

"He's not the only one here." Bernice smiled as she said this, but she was dead serious.

Doc just shook her head and looked at me. She didn't come for a fight or mean anything by the statement, so she chatted with me for awhile and then left.

After she left, I got a protracted lecture about how I wasn't the only one in the house, and "Ms. King" acted as though she didn't care about anyone else but me. There was much more behind this interaction. The long standing mistrust of Doc and the rather terse exchanges between the two of them during the days I first went down with Legionnaire's disease aroused Bernice's ire. However, I think the most disturbing thing was she had finally understood I had a life that didn't include her, and I had no intention of reconciling. She believed my mom and Rod were supportive of and complicit in my decision to end our marriage. It simply wasn't true. All hell broke loose. My mom's simple statement brought back all the hurt and pain of losing me several months before and the realization that there wouldn't be any reconciliation.

This entire episode happened because of my scrambled brain. My hard drive had been burned from the persistent fever. In the days following my discharge from St. Luke's, I had given her the password to my online account. This provided an open book and unintended disclosure of some of my private matters since our breakup. She read my e-mail and was surprised and angered by some of the messages. I learned a couple of valuable lessons. One must always be extremely careful about what is written in e-mail and even more thoughtful about the recipients on e-mail. From that point forward, I would subscribe to the adage that if you wouldn't be comfortable reading one of your e-mails in the newspaper, then you shouldn't write it online.

All this made for some very tense moments during my Indiana-based recovery. I needed to focus on learning to talk and getting stronger. This situation thoroughly strengthened my resolve to gain my independence and

Never Better

get back to Houston. Years later Doc and Bernice made their peace and got along well. Although that particular time was awkward, there were other events that made the time enjoyable. One of those was a visit from an old friend.

My friend, Jean, who worked with me at LNIMC, came for a visit one sunny morning. When we worked together, our cubicles were within close proximity. We teased each other endlessly most days but managed to get our share of real investment work done. I found and won deals, while she closed them after we won. She did her job thoroughly and professionally. When it came to making sure all the documents and requirements were fulfilled, our deals were closed right.

Jean played NCAA Division I women's basketball. I always admired her and loved to hear the stories of her playing ball. Jean had the same competitive spirit I had. She loved physical fitness and played volleyball and softball in her leisure time. Sports talk crowded our conversations. After we'd worked together for a while, I told her she was my "FWW": favorite white woman.

She came up with a name for me. I became "BH": black hunk. Obviously, I agreed with her on the appropriateness of that nickname. I made sure she knew that I thought the description fit me perfectly.

It thrilled me to see her walking up to the door, grinning from ear to ear.

"Hey, BH! How you doing, honey?"

"Hey...Jean."

"Man, you ain't nuthin' but skin and bones, BH. You better lift some weights." She giggled and kissed me on the check. Jean's visit warmed my heart. She filled me in on the latest with all the guys I worked with at LNIMC. She had finished her degree and now generated her own investments. What a story of determination. I took careful note of it. God had put people around me who loved me, lifted my spirits, and inspired me.

Before she left, we posed for a picture. She put her arm around my waist, pinched my behind, and laughed. She was just plain naughty. It was all in good fun. "Damn, you need some meat on these bones, BH!" Only she could get away with that behavior.

That Indiana October not only brought visitors, it also brought crisp autumn nights and Friday night high school football games. My children's high school homecoming game was upon us. This homecoming would be special for my kids. Geoffrey played on the football team, and Kristi had been nominated to homecoming court.

I believed she would be queen. She stood a tad over five feet tall and weighed just over one hundred pounds. She had a natural beauty with a striking, girl-next-door wholesome look. For years, I kept a picture of Doc

113

at sixteen years old. The resemblance between the two astonished me. They both were fair-colored with long, straight, black hair. Some black men called women with these characteristics "redbones" or "high yellow." Whatever the label, Kristi resembled a doll.

I had a mantra that whole week. "She…is…gon…na…win!" Kristi was gorgeous and smart. She would become the salutatorian of her class and winner of several academic awards. These honors came because she studied hard and all but eschewed any social life. She never considered herself special at all. She gasped and clutched herself when homecoming night came, and my prediction came true. I cheered as best as I could. Then the tears started to roll as I realized I just about missed all of this. Kristi had been there when I needed her. Had she not come to Houston, I'm convinced I could have died alone in my apartment. She deserved to be homecoming queen.

What a great forty-fourth birthday present for me. A huge party in my honor drew well-wishers from all over. That night, I felt as happy as I could, because I learned I had many friends. It seemed they all wanted me to stay in Fort Wayne. A couple people suggested I go on disability, collect benefits, and never work again. Price Love would turn over in his grave if I sought the easy way out and didn't work to support myself and my extended family. I could see the pity in their eyes, and I didn't like it one bit. While I enjoyed the evening, it stoked my desire to get back to work.

The most astonishing October news came just before the birthday party. The Mayo Clinic in Rochester, Minnesota, had agreed to let me be examined by its staff. Mayo Clinic is the largest group practice in the world with literally thousands of doctors on staff from every medical specialty. It is world renowned for excellence in research, medical breakthroughs, and patient care. I hoped to go there to find a miracle cure for dysarthria. We booked a flight to Minneapolis/St. Paul and made the short drive to Rochester during the last week of the month.

The Mayo Clinic is actually an urban campus with several buildings, so patients and their family members or friends go from building to building depending on the test or procedure they were having done. There were people from all over the country in Rochester for treatment and or analysis. So many people looked feeble and sick. A gray heaviness hovered over the campus. Many people, like me, had come there for a miracle cure. Even though listening to the various stories of the other patients or their family members in the waiting areas made me sad, I felt very fortunate to have the opportunity to be examined by some of best physicians in the world. No one in my family or circle of friends had ever even thought about seeking treatment at the Mayo Clinic. That "first" is one I would have rather not experienced for many reasons.

I had a battery of tests over two or three days as an outpatient. Many were the exact same tests I had in Houston's Medical Center such as MRI and CT scan. I had become an old pro at being poked and prodded, so I wasn't fazed too much by any of it. However, the spinal tap got my full attention. The procedure is essentially all about having spinal fluid extracted by a large needle while the patient lies completely still. It took a lot of visualization about riding my bike in the Texas countryside to block out the thought of a huge needle being injected directly into my back to draw spinal fluid. The test went fine, but it scared me to death.

I looked forward to the visit with the speech specialist. He listened to me talk and had me attempt the same exercises Sarah did back in Houston. In order to give this doctor a feel for how I used to sound, we brought my cell phone and played my recorded outgoing message. Little did I know when I recorded that greeting the previous year, I would have to use it later to prove that I, at one time, had normal speech patterns. That doctor couldn't do anything about my condition.

In fact, there were no new revelations from the Mayo Clinic at all. This was a major letdown for me. I learned there is no cure for dysarthria or ataxia. The most disappointing proclamation by the doctor who looked at the MRI of my brain was that I had no permanent brain damage. How could that be? I could barely talk, had trouble swallowing, had memory loss, and had ambulatory issues. To add insult to injury, later I learned that my health insurance wouldn't pay for the visit to the Mayo Clinic even though my caseworker shared we had authorization. I wanted to get back to Indiana in the worst way to continue my personal mission to make a comeback.

When we got back to Fort Wayne, Kathleen and I spoke by phone.

"Wow, Cal, you sound better. How are things going?"

I agreed with her even though a notepad and pencil continued to be my primary mode of communication. While I wouldn't be giving speeches at rallies, I began to speak some words with a little more clarity. The drooling persisted, as well as speaking one syllable at a time. However, the words were starting to come back, one by one.

No matter what anyone said, I had made up my mind to win this fight. Kathleen asked me how things were going, but I heard the unasked question: do you think you'll come back? I let her know exactly where I stood with respect to returning to Houston or not.

"I...plan...to...come... back...to...work..."

"Cal, just take it easy and get better. You don't have to worry about the Client Care Center. It will be there when you get back."

Kathleen knew about my very competitive character, but she had confided in Lois she wasn't sure I would work again. I believe she understood I had a ways to go, but she committed to hanging in there with me and giving me enough time and space to fight my way back. She believed in me.

A couple days later, Rod called to talk to me about the upcoming Indianapolis Colts game against the Detroit Lions. This trip would get me off the living room couch, out of the house, and back into some semblance of normalcy. When I got to Rod's house, he squeezed me so tight it took my breath away. There had been a serious juxtaposition. Rod had ascended to the role of the alpha male of our family. He had become the bigger and stronger brother looking out for me and the rest of his family. I would always be Cashflow, but for the time being, Doc and my sisters would look to him for direction and security going forward. So would I.

When we got to the RCA Dome, I got hugs from all the other season ticket holders in our section. They were my Colts family. Rod had shared the story about my journey with Legionnaire's disease. I gave everyone the famous Cal smile. Every one of my friends had a notepad and pen so they could "talk" to me during the game. They all waved their pads at me and laughed. This gesture warmed my heart. The tears started to flow, and I clutched my brother's arm. The Colts proceeded to put on a show and thrashed the Lions. This victory ushered in a perfect closing to a special Indiana October.

Chapter 16
FURRY FRIENDS

Pops's Return

I HAD A MORNING RITUAL OF eating breakfast, taking a nap, practicing the clicking sound, reading, and then taking a walk. After finishing this routine, I made my way to the living room couch, which had become my primary post. The tan, plush cloth couch sat in front of a large picture window that ushered in continuous sunshine and a view of the outside world. Day after day after day in autumn 2000, I sat on that couch contemplating my life.

I had an unlikely companion who loved soaking up the living room sun as much as I did. We met seven years earlier, one day after I came home from work. As I walked through the front entrance my wife emerged from behind the door scantily clad, holding a small gray ball of fur. It looked up at me with nervous eyes.

"Mew."

"What is this?"

"Isn't he cute? Can we keep him?"

"You know I don't want another cat!"

"But he's so cute. He is a twin. Our friend, Vickie, gave him to me. Her daughter, Stacy, has the other one. "

"He's cute now, but he'll grow into a big cat, and no one will take care of him. I ain't taking care of this cat."

"Please!"

A couple days later, the fur ball had moved in for good. I had given him a name: Marbles. Marbles was a domestic short-hair cat with a shiny gray coat. Over the next seven years, he grew from a little fur ball into a sixteen-pound tomcat.

Marbles loved the whole family except me. Maybe he sensed he wasn't on my favorites list. I never brushed him or loved on him the way Kristi or the others did. My interactions with him had been largely limited to yelling

117

commands to get out of my way or to go to the basement where he spent every night.

There are dog people and cat people. I was neither. In fact, for years, I didn't like cats at all and never saw myself owning one. I had a vivid memory of the weekend night during high school when my best friend Anthony, his brother Melvin, and our buddy Darrell rode around in my 1962 Volkswagen Beetle looking to frighten cats. We played the music loud and talked about our distaste for cats in my black VW, which had beads strung across the back window and seats covered with a wildly printed contact paper. Our big afros and the VW Bug made us look like we were part of the Mod Squad.

As we cruised along, flashing patrol car lights suddenly appeared behind us. The squad car moved to the middle of the road. The officers pointed a bright flood light into the back of my VW.

"Damn, it's my Pops." My friends snickered

"Uh-oh, Calvin. Yo' daddy is gonna whip yo' ass!"

I fumed but pulled over and got out of the car. Pops met me at the rear of my car. He looked down at me intently.

"Where you going, boy?"

"Nowhere, Pops. We're just riding around."

"You boys ain't drinking, are you?"

"No, sir!"

"You better not be!"

"Come on, Pops, you know better. This is so embarrassing, man. My friends are cracking on me." He knew Anthony and I were serious athletes. We never drank or smoked marijuana like a lot of other guys our age were doing. I couldn't say the same for Melvin or our friend Darrell. They were the wild pair in our foursome.

"Okay, be careful out here, son. These streets is bad, I'm just lookin' out for you."

Pops stopped me several times in the same manner. It embarrassed and irritated me each time. I knew he only stopped me because he wanted to keep me safe and out of trouble. That particular traffic stop prevented a cat from being tortured. Our search for cats had come to an abrupt end.

I can only guess Marbles sensed something had changed when, after many months of being gone, I returned to his house and perched on the living room couch every day. Only now, I wasn't yelling at him to get away. I couldn't. Soon, he began to take up positions where he could watch me closely and sunbathe. We had become friends, Marbles and me. It was okay.

Marbles sat with me the first day Pops came to visit after I returned to Indiana from Houston. He stared at Pops for awhile, but then quickly disappeared. He didn't like strangers and would leave my side whenever visitors called.

Pops had crossed my mind a lot during those days. I had been doing a lot of soul-searching and reflecting on the past. He played a big part in my past. I asked myself so many "what if" questions as Marbles and I sat in the living room enjoying the sunlight every day.

Some of those questions naturally centered on my father and his influence on my life. I had learned so much from him. He had worked hard to give us a good life. Pops promised to put me through college. I relied on that promise. In the fall of my junior year of high school, representatives from a historically black college in Missouri had a booth at my high school's college fair. This school had a strong computer technology program that caught my attention. When the time came to leave for school, Pops was long gone along with my dream of attending college away from home.

Would I be on this couch struggling to talk to him and fighting to overcome an unspeakable sickness had I gone away to school instead of working at a local steak house? I would never know for sure. I certainly would have never been the one chosen by Don Eckrich and never set on this path over twenty years before that ultimately led me to this point.

None of this sickness or its challenges was Pops's fault. We had long since made our peace. I felt overjoyed to see him that day. I'm not even sure he fully understood what had happened to me. Neither one of us had much to say, but I knew he loved me and worried about whether I could recover.

Our reconnection occurred in the mid-1980s. It developed slowly. I only reluctantly forgave him for the hurt he caused all of us ten years before. When I finally had the opportunity to pour out my heart to him on a cool fall afternoon as we sat on my front porch, his reaction stunned me. I learned he didn't realize I had any hard feelings toward him related to the disintegration of our family.

Over the years following his divorce from my mother, I had grown more and more disappointed with him. My disappointment turned to resentment, as I saw him go from woman to woman, and in and out of marriages. All the while, I had taken his place as the person making sure Doc had everything she needed to live a comfortable life. I watched him move from place to place and file for bankruptcy twice. He never had any money and only came around when he wanted to borrow cash from me. He didn't remember my birthdays or any other specials days in my life. He just wasn't there, especially for my little brother. I was angry with him for not being around to teach Rod the good lessons he taught me. I was angry with him for being a stranger to my little brother.

He told a different story. He shared that he had paid support and made sure we had what we needed after he left. I never saw any evidence of that. I didn't believe him, but I had fully committed to forgiving him, so I could free myself from all the terrible feelings I had inside about the things he did.

I had a hard time reconciling all that behavior compared to what I learned from him as a youngster. Back then, he worked hard, saved money, and was an excellent provider. He could put me in my place by helping me to remember my roots. Where did that man go? I caught a glimpse of him one day while working at Lincoln Life. By this time, Pops had retired and performed odd security jobs to supplement his fixed income. I had been promoted to second vice president and had worked hard on building a polished and sophisticated image.

One day, I had gone to lunch with a few colleagues and parked my car in Lincoln's lot as we returned. Pops worked for the security company that patrolled Lincoln's parking lots. That day, as my friends and I walked back to the office, a voice boomed out behind us.

"Hey, boy!" Everyone turned around to look. I immediately knew the voice and the name.

Oh my God. It was Pops! *He called me "boy" in front of these people.* I felt flushed and stammered, "Hey, it's my dad." I introduced him to my friends and told them to go ahead.

"How you doing, son?"

"Doing good, Pops. How you doing? It's good to see you."

"Shit, son, they got me sitting here, and it's killing my back, but it's okay." Over the years, he had developed chronic back problems, and long periods of sitting were almost unbearable. "You lookin' good, boy. I'm so proud of you. Keep up the good work. Never forget where you came from. Make sure you get your rest and look out for my grandkids. They'll be grown before you know it."

I had made him proud. That felt good.

Marbles came back. He stared at me and Pops for a while and then found a spot drenched in sunlight. He lay down in the sun, looked over at us, yawned and spoke.

"Meow."

Pops laughed and said, "is that your furry friend?" Marbles put his head down and went to sleep. We were three friends just chillin' in the living room.

Chapter 17
So Now What?

Deciding to Live Life on My Own Terms

VOTERS WERE EXCITED IN HOUSTON AND Texas in general, because the long awaited 2000 Presidential election loomed. Texas's native son and governor, George W. Bush, poised for a struggle in the early November battle against Vice President Al Gore to gain the presidency being vacated by Bill Clinton. Election night found me back in Houston. My friend Laura and I sat in a pizza joint to watch the election returns and debate the virtues of liberal and conservative politics. It wasn't much of a debate. She waxed poetically about how great Al Gore was and how stupid George Bush was. I nodded, shook my head violently, or muttered a few syllables and drooled, depending on the topic. My long career in banking and finance drove my support of Bush's conservative agenda, while young and idealistic Laura staunchly supported Gore.

We spent the entire evening watching the talking heads paint the map of the United States red or blue only to have the race end in a draw. Who knew which direction the country would take? The symbolism of that day didn't escape me. The nation had voted, and yet the outcome hung in the balance with no clear-cut end result.

Now what? This pervasive question just wouldn't go away quietly for my country or me. From the moment I took the sun-drenched ride home from St. Luke's hospital until the beautiful Indiana autumn colors slowly drifted away to a dreary brown and gray November, the question of what would become of my life persisted. All the people around me wanted to know what I would decide to do.

All the while, a great unshakable paradox engulfed me. Confusion about the recent turn of events filled my mind. Therefore, I could not be sure about what the future held. The origin of this confusion started and ended with my quest to understand why all this had happened. At the same time, I always knew one answer with certainty: I expected to get better and make a comeback. Where would that comeback lead me? I had no clue.

People would be disappointed if I didn't recover. I had never liked disappointing anyone. However, I learned a new life lesson during this challenging journey. From now on, there would be times I would disappoint people in my life. I discovered that I could now live with disappointing others sometimes.

The people around me had their own reasons, agendas, and motivations for me to recover and exist in their spheres of life. That way, they could have me do what they wanted me to do, be what they wanted, or be where they wanted me to be. It's a selfish thing we all do. Sometimes we want those around us to follow the path we want them to follow instead of following the path ordained for them. Our selfishness can stifle creativity, choke out greatness, and circumvent winning opportunities for others, all in the name of getting our way or unjustly imposing our will. I had been as guilty of that atrocity as anyone else.

Now, I had my own reasons for deciding I would fight the fight of overcoming the effects of Legionnaire's disease. One might think it centered on the good and noble idea of overcoming the physical adversity presented by a terrible illness and disability. Yes, that was a part of it, but I wanted to regain complete independence and tried to figure out where I should go and what I should do on my own terms. In short, my goal became all about living on my own terms for the rest of my life.

Then there were the spiritual questions that confused me. Others preached to me or tried to force me into quick answers. What was God's will for my life? Did he slow me down to get my attention? Was he punishing me for not going into the ministry? Was this situation thrust upon me to help others? Did this happen because of sin in my life? Many had asked these questions, including me.

Really, no one had clear or quick answers. Christians have a way of burying their wounded sometimes. They can be self-righteous and holier than thou. It troubled me and made me angry that some implied I was in trouble with God, and he "did" this to me. Now, I fully rejected that notion even though for many years I too had been one of the poster children pretending to be holy and sinless despite harboring dirty little secrets.

Instead, I listened for that small quiet voice to whisper the answers to my spirit. I read my Bible and prayed for comfort and direction. I listened to gospel music to usher peace into my spirit and soul. In time, I drew the conclusion that God would reveal the answers to me in his time, not mine. He would wink at me, and I would know his plans for me. So I stopped worrying about figuring it all out right then. For now, the "why" of this belonged to God. It was his thing; not mine.

A line in a song we used to sing in church when as I grew up says, "*He may not come when you want him, but he's always right on time.*"

I convinced myself God would help me understand what my life should be as the days unfolded. I worked on quieting myself. That revelation liberated my mind and spirit and quieted my soul.

With that settled, instead of *now what?* the question that persisted in my mind was *did I survive this only to go back to being unhappy in any aspect of my life?* I knew my answer to that question. It was easy. Of course not! One thing I was certain of, the time had come to make the changes God had given me the ability and intellect to handle myself. What I didn't know was exactly how to affect some of the changes in part due to the disabilities that now afflicted me.

The stories of my Gramps, Price Love, kept playing out in my head. His legacy of working for a living, providing for his kin folk, and saving for the future had become part of my fiber. I had worked somebody's job for thirty years. Able-bodied men who refused to work or who let their women take care of them are lazy bastards—disgraceful and worthless in my opinion. I despised them and would never be counted among those ranks. I refused to succumb to a life of disability or laziness if I overcame the effects of this awful disease.

Although I could afford to stay home now and never work again, I didn't want to. I wasn't rich, but I had done well and been frugal over the years. I practiced good stewardship over the assets given to me. We gave a tenth of our earnings to the church, paid cash for many purchases, lived within our means, and kept credit usage to a minimum. I had worked hard and saved enough money to put my kids through college, pay off the mortgage on my house, and put aside liquid assets and savings.

However, there was a financial implication for leaving my company I wanted to avoid. I had been offered an attractive compensation package commensurate with my position. Part of the deal included a "sign-on" bonus, which I would forfeit should I leave the company within one year. Since I had joined the company in February 2000, according to the agreement, I had to stay there until February 2001 to retain the bonus.

I considered this provision as I willed myself to get well enough to return to Houston and get back on the job. In addition, a voice in my head told me that quitting my job and moving back to Indiana would mean I had failed at my attempt to break away from my comfort zones and compete with executives anywhere in the country. I simply could not live with that failure.

I hated losing at anything. It didn't matter what the competition might be, including doing my job. I couldn't be a failure at all.

At forty-four years old, I had reached the prime income earning period in my life. If I could regain my ability to speak and care for myself, I'd be fine. And yet, as I worked through these mental obstacles, the thought crossed my mind that I had no choice but to go back to Houston to work. No other company would want me because of my brokenness. I could send my resume, which extolled all my skills and competencies, but once I showed up for the interview, looking frail and speech-impaired, that would be it. The thought of this caused me to cry many, many times.

Independence all but consumed my mind. I had experienced a taste of being away from everyone I'd grown up with. Even though I had been lonely at times, I found myself longing for life in Houston. It was a cool life, my life in Houston. I wanted to feel that vibe again. On top of that, I wondered about Michele. The opportunity to put the whole *now what* question behind me once and for all came as I returned to Houston for follow-up visits with Dr. Kevorkian and Dr. Tiwari. The feeling of the big city vibe I enjoyed so much inched closer.

My chance to get the vibe back rested on getting a couple of quick wins. The first victory would be getting permission to drive. The second would be obtaining a release to return to work. I got both victories in inverse order.

During the short ride to the medical center to see Dr. K, I felt nervous but hopeful. He put me through several dexterity tests. No sweat. I still told my limbs to move, but my dexterity had been slowly getting better. My fine motor skills had not seen fit to return to their pre-August state, but they were sufficient. I still couldn't put in contact lenses or drive screws, but I could write and had better control of my fingers and hands. I only dropped things occasionally now. My balance and gait still wobbled if I didn't take my time and really concentrate.

"How is the swallowing and drinking going?" Dr. K asked.

This problem persisted and hadn't really improved. Dysarthria and ataxia had severely weakened my jaw muscles, and my tongue movement was still very limited at best. On top of that, I drooled nearly every time I tried to speak. I kept a handkerchief or bandanna with me at all times to wipe my chin.

Curiously, the only way I could drink without uncontrollable coughing and choking was by using a straw. Even using a straw didn't mean sure-fire success. In addition, if I didn't take very small bites and chew extremely slowly, foods with a heavy or thick consistency were nearly impossible to eat. Every meal was an adventure in concentrating on not choking.

"It…is…hard…but…I…try…real…ly…hard."

He repeated something he said eight weeks earlier. "You've got to slow down, Mr. King. It would be a shame to survive this and choke to death. Take your time."

"O...kay." I didn't know it then, but these conditions would get somewhat better over time. However, I would have to be very careful eating and drinking for the rest of my life. Even the simple task of chewing gum proved impossible up to this point.

"Do you have any questions?"

"How...long...be...fore...I...get...bet...ter?"

"You are making very good progress. Your hand/eye coordination is better and your ambulatory movements have shown improvement. This will take some time. Just be very patient. No need to rush."

I couldn't have disagreed more. The time came for the sixty-four-dollar question. Nervousness nearly prevented me from asking about work. Dr. K's somber demeanor as he exhorted me to take it easy didn't help my confidence at all.

"Can...I...go...to...work?" I got it out and then my heart stopped because Dr. K immediately shook his head several times as he let out a heavy, measured sigh.

"You know, people are so mean. They won't understand all you've been through, and you would have a very, very difficult time. I'm not sure you can ever handle that again."

I was devastated. It was one thing for other people to plant seeds of doubt, but entirely another for my doctor to think I should never work again. Out of the corner of my eye, I thought I saw Bernice nod her head in affirmation, but she didn't say a word. I knew she would love this disposition. She wanted desperately for me to give up the whole Houston experiment and move back to Indiana to be with her. Even though she had been kind and cared for me, returning to Indiana permanently wasn't in my plans. In addition, we had been fighting over my previous indiscretions quite a bit even though all that behavior didn't really matter at that point. Moreover, she disliked my family more than ever now. I couldn't handle that drama anymore and would figure out how to solve that problem later. This was all about me and my ability to move forward. I just stared at him as he continued. My body temperature began to rise and heat rushed to my head. The room spun around.

"The people in your family care about you and are nurturing. You wouldn't have the benefit of that at work. I don't think it's a good idea. Your job is a high-visibility job that takes a lot of energy. You've been through so much. I don't think you can handle that pace and stress anymore."

A long, pregnant pause filled the room. The seconds that passed before I spoke up seemed like weeks. My mind raced.

I had run road races and marathons as Team Fudd's Stallion. I'd rode literally thousands of miles on my bike doing tours and riding for fun. These physical exercises took a special kind of mental toughness, intestinal fortitude, and an uncommon drive to succeed. Those attributes carried over to every aspect of my life. I was a winner. Yes, I got tired very easily now after jogging a few blocks, but I refused to stop living life to the fullest. Price Love's grandson won at everything. Doc's golden child had gold to mine. My destiny lay in getting back to work.

The whispers and suggestions about going on permanent disability and collecting a monthly income from the government came rushing to my mind. Maybe Dr. Kevorkian was right after all. Maybe the time had come to file a claim on my disability policy.

Just as quickly as those thoughts came, I summarily rejected them all. I could never be a slave to Uncle Sam or live with the stigma of needing a handout every month or offering proof that I was an invalid. I had been an aspiring business executive, used to relying on skills and competencies to earn a comfortable living. Besides, going on disability meant the equivalent of capitulating to Legionnaire's disease. I would never do that. I had the heart of a stallion, and I would never be a quitter.

"I…think…I…can…do…it." I could, and I would. Dr. K looked at me intently and shook his head again.

"I don't think this is a good idea at all. Perhaps you can try it part-time for a while and see how it goes."

It was all I needed to hear. He gave me permission to start half days in December. That would give me nearly a month to work on speech, stamina, and dexterity. One down, one to go.

A few days later, I traveled to another doctor's office. My neurologist, Dr. Tiwari, moved into my personal space with a smiling face. She was always so pleasant and happy. I enjoyed seeing her very much. She was adorable!

"Touch your right finger to your nose, like this. Now, your left."

That motion came easily. I smiled after completing the command.

"Okay, follow my finger with your eyes." She moved her finger in front of my face from left to right. My eyes followed closely.

She tapped my knees, shins, and heels with a soft mallet. My legs moved upon each impact. She seemed pleased with the resultant involuntary responses.

"Now, walk over there and back."

I concentrated as hard as I could to walk straight and keep my balance. I exercised an abundance of care with walking just as I did with drinking, eating and swallowing. I showed the outside world a straight and proud walk, but in actuality, I had big trouble balancing and walking with a natural gait. I had to take my time and concentrate really hard for months to come whenever I walked. I kept that challenge as a personal secret from everyone.

"Good! Things seemed to going well, Mr. King. What questions do you have?"

"Will...I...ev...er ...be ... ...able ...to ...talk ...nor ...mal ...ly ...a ...gain?"

"The brain is a complicated thing. You've made more progress than expected. Sometimes it finds a way to rewire itself. Only time will tell. How is the speech therapy going?"

"O...kay. There...are ...some ...words ...I...can't ...say."

"Just keep practicing. What else is going on?"

"Can't...stop...drool...ing." Of course, she could see this embarrassed me.

"Don't worry. I can give you something to dry that up."

She stared at me intently with big brown eyes so as to figure out exactly what my thoughts were.

Get it out, you dummy, I said to myself. "When...can ...I ...drive?"

"Your coordination seems to be acceptable. I think you'd be okay driving."

There it was, the double victory I had been diligently seeking! I hadn't driven my car in three months. The next day, things would change.

Since early August, others had driven my car. I hadn't. I adjusted all the mirrors and the driver's seat. Those adjustments were easy enough. But as I inhaled the aroma of the leather upholstery, I couldn't believe how nervous this pending adventure made me. I steadied myself from trembling and wiped my sweating palms on my trousers. I gripped the steering wheel like I did when I took driver's training twenty-five years before. My hands were firmly positioned at ten and two o'clock. I backed out of my parking space and made my way out of the garage. There were no clouds that November morning. It looked like a perfect day for a Sunday drive, though it was midweek. I had purposely waited until late morning. Rush hour would be long past. I wouldn't have to worry about crazies racing to their workstations or subjecting myself to road rage. I had no specific destination at all. I just wanted to drive.

I started the drive with winding around the side streets in West U. My SUV was more powerful than I remembered. A fierce battle to keep it properly aimed on the road ensued. I kept a white-knuckled grip on the wheel. Clearly I'd have to practice quite a bit before I could drive from home to my office. Maybe I could make it to the Allen Parkway campus near downtown. So I pointed the car towards the campus. The people passing me had to be frustrated by how slowly and awfully I drove. After getting passed by several cars and receiving numerous horn honks, I pulled onto a side street to gather myself.

I decided to call Michele. I had missed her terribly and could finally see her again. What would she think when she saw me? I had hoped I wouldn't have to worry about that. I thought we had made a connection before I got sick. I dialed her number from my cell phone with trembling fingers.

"Hi...this...is...Cal."

"Cal! How are you? Oh my God! How are you? I've been so worried. I miss you, man. Where are you?"

"In...Hous...ton. I...am...dri...ving...my...car. Can...I...come...to... see you?" Drool ran down my chin, and I retrieved my handkerchief to wipe it away. Maybe this wasn't such a good idea after all. "I...can't...com...in... side. Can...you...come...out...side?"

"Sure, sweetie. Call me when you get here."

I asked Michele to meet me outside, because I didn't want to go on campus at all. Kathleen would be busy, and I didn't want anyone else to see me yet. I still looked like death warmed over, and I drooled badly. No sense showing that picture to six thousand fellow employees and subjecting myself to stares. I wasn't quite ready to face the world just yet.

Michele walked toward the Italian restaurant parking lot where I nervously waited, across the street from the sprawling five-building downtown complex. Her striking, tall, and angular figure moved effortlessly. Her sharp hazel eyes trained on me. Once she got closer, her smiling face transitioned to a face veiled in disbelief and concern.

"I missed you so much." Her embrace and gentle kiss comforted me. She had last seen me three months ago for a late-night dinner after I returned from Chicago. Little did I know then, when she told me I didn't look so good and that I should rest, how close I came to never seeing her again.

"I...mi—mi—missed...you...too." I had trouble saying the letters "s" and "t." I trembled and had more difficulty getting even simple syllables out. A long line of drool made its way down my chin. I quickly pulled out my hanky and kept it over my mouth for the remainder of our short conversation.

"I tried to keep up with what was going on with you through Lois, but I really don't know everything that happened, Cal."

"Leg...ion...naire's...di...sease. I...tried...to...tell...you...on...the... phone."

"Oh my God, I know, Cal!" She held me tight, and the smell of her perfume filled my senses. I melted in her embrace and almost drooled on her shoulder. She had figured out what I had told her over the phone but had also heard the whole story from Lois.

"It…real…ly…messed…me…up…but…I…am…go…ing…bac…to… work. I…can…drive…my…car…now…so…I…will…be…okay."

"Have you seen anyone else from work?"

"Ju—ju—just…" The words wouldn't come out of my mouth as fast as they were moving in my head.

"Kath…leen…and…Lau…ra. Wan…ted…to…see…Jim…but…I… am…not…go…ing…to…the… cam…pus."

"Oh. That makes sense."

"Can…I…keep…in…t—touch…with…you?"

"Sure, Cal, I would like that. Are you back here for good now? We've got places to go, man!"

"I…will…be…in…a…cou…ple…weeks." It was a bold prediction on my part but one I planned to make good on. She kissed my lips tenderly and squeezed me tight.

"I love you, Cal."

"No…you…don't…love…me." She couldn't. It was much too soon for that.

The meeting with Michele was my first encounter with someone from Houston outside of my circle of friends from Indiana. Because we had formed a bond, it probably had gone as well as it could have. Michele's eyes danced as she gave me a goodbye glance, but her initial look of concern is one I would see over and over again from people in the days ahead. I would come to expect this and had to learn how to put people at ease with me.

When I returned to Fort Wayne a few days later, I met my friends from Team Fudd at Foster Park. Although I knew I couldn't keep up with Fudd over a long distance, I thought I could run a few miles.

The Hawk had returned to Indiana with its snow and stiff wind. This wasn't optimal weather for the beginning of a training comeback, but it would have to do. Slowly but surely, the whole group arrived one car at a time until we had a full contingent of Fudd. There were hugs all around. Before long, we were running on the snow-covered roads around the golf course. We headed toward a well-traveled running lane and greenway.

My heart pounded so loudly, I thought the whole gang could hear it. My lungs burned as I gulped in cold air. They didn't seem to have the same capacity to power me through the rigorous workouts. They simply didn't function at the level of oxygen intake I had become accustomed to. After a couple miles, my right shoelace wiggled loose. I had grown very tired. The shoelace made a great excuse to stop everyone so I could rest. I got several back slaps and pats on the rear. I was back!

The group planned to run seven or eight miles. I figured I could make it three. But first, the business of my shoelace needed settling. I looked over at Linda.

"Would...you. .....tie...my...shoe?" It took me about thirty seconds to ask Linda for help because of exhaustion from the run.

She kneeled down in the snow and gently retied my shoe. "There you go, Cal!" She beamed a huge smile at me. No wonder her Fudd nickname was Princess.

Linda shared this kind gesture. When I couldn't do for myself, someone was right there to help me. No one on Team Fudd teased me or scoffed because I couldn't keep up or go the distance. They didn't make fun of me for having a slightly lopsided gait or for not being able to talk during the run anymore. They didn't laugh at the frozen drool on my chin. When I reached a point of distress, they all stopped.

So many times I had been in this park and ran past people who were fat, slow, or not "normal." I used to laugh at them to myself or make fun of them. What came to mind at that moment when Linda showed the act of kindness was the affirmation I would never again make fun of anyone with a disability or for not fitting the perfect mold society thinks one should fit. Certainly, if someone overweight or with a disability had enough courage and strength to overcome the challenges of life, that in and of itself was a miracle. Who am I to make fun of them? Besides, I could totally relate now.

The team prepared to resume the training run. I'd had enough. I waved them on. I jogged back to my car and waited for them to finish the workout.

Now what? A greasy breakfast at our favorite post-run restaurant. It was like old times.

Chapter 18

YEA, THOUGH I WALK THROUGH
THE VALLEY OF THE SHADOW...

Overcoming Fear

IT'S INTERESTING TO ME THAT AFTER years of being a Gavin-trained, staunch Republican, I realized that the two presidents I admired the most in this century were both Democrats. Lyndon Johnson's Great Society drove unprecedented change in our country, and Franklin Roosevelt's leadership during the Great Depression and World War II inspired the nation to overcome gut-wrenching adversity.

Johnson's Great Society programs, forced into existence in part by the Civil Rights movement, were responsible for me going to Indian Village School. Those programs opened the door for my parents to buy a house on Fort Wayne's predominantly white south side in the 1960s, without the intervention of unfair housing practices. Even though those events put me on a collision course with destiny, the Roosevelt story in particular intrigued me for a couple reasons.

First, I admired Roosevelt because he overcame the effects of polio to lead our country. His dealing with the resultant disability was so successful that many people didn't know he had extreme difficulty standing and walking. He achieved this feat even though he held the most powerful office in the world, subjected to constant media coverage and scrutiny. Second, he took full advantage of the relatively new media of radio to share his New Deal with a smooth, comforting, and reassuring tone. I had been told that I had a smooth and comforting voice too. That had changed. Nevertheless, I felt if Roosevelt could lead the nation while dealing with polio, I could run a call center in spite of my disability.

Roosevelt's "Fireside Chats"—enabled by the "new" technology of radio—were powerful during the 1930s. There were a couple of lines from his many speeches that rattled in my head during the first week of December

2000. But the Roosevelt quote that meant the most to me on the morning of December 4 came from his first Inaugural Address. Our nation was gripped with fear of what lay ahead in the wake of devastation and despair caused by the Great Depression. Roosevelt said, "The only thing we have to fear is fear itself."

December 4 would be a pivotal day for me. I would return to work. The thought of my return frightened me to the core. I hadn't worked in four months. It felt like starting a new job. Only now, I wasn't smooth enough to do what the youth pastor told me to do years before.

"Fake it till you make it!"

Now, each time I opened my mouth to speak, the struggle would be apparent to others. I had already been in public places and seen the reaction from people that said, "What's wrong with this guy? Is he retarded? Is he hearing impaired?" Those looks of concern crushed my ego and spirit.

On top of that, I had a skinny frame and a sunken face. The brash and arrogant Cal focused solely on making a name for himself had vanished. He had been replaced with a more patient and compassionate person who valued life and relationships. The new Cal contemplated a big case of fear, worry, insecurities about personal appearance, and a deep concern about other people's acceptance of his disability. This Cal had begun a search for acceptance in a peaceful environment.

Dr. Kevorkian had said people were mean and that I might have a hard time handling all that. I didn't want this day in December to be like the December "Day of Infamy" Roosevelt described to a nervous nation. The Japanese had bombed Pearl Harbor, on his watch, on a quiet December morning in 1941. What if, after all the talk of wanting to return to work and projecting confidence in doing so, the whole thing blew up in my face and I couldn't do it? What if my enemies of disability, fear and doubt, dropped bombs in the quiet harbor of my dreams and sunk my fragile comeback attempt?

As the day approached, my thoughts moved from politics and its rhetoric to my spiritual roots. Politics couldn't help me with this. Charm, affability, skills, talent, smooth talking, or any other personal attributes I heavily relied on previously had not saved me from nearly succumbing to Legionnaire's disease. I learned I needed God's help to get through each and every day, including the dark days in August I couldn't even remember. I turned to my faith in an attempt to overcome the fear and to take the steps necessary to get past the tragedy of illness that nearly claimed my life. A familiar scripture began to be imprinted on my mind night and day:

"The LORD is my shepherd; I shall not want. He maketh me to lie down in green pastures: he leadeth me beside the still waters. He restoreth my soul: he

leadeth me in the paths of righteousness for his name's sake. Yea, though I walk through the valley of the shadow of death, I will fear no evil: for thou art with me; thy rod and thy staff they comfort me. Thou preparest a table before me in the presence of mine enemies: thou anointest my head with oil; my cup runneth over. Surely goodness and mercy shall follow me all the days of my life: and I will dwell in the house of the LORD forever." (Psalms 23 KJV)

Surviving and recovering from Legionnaire's disease had been four months of walking through the valley of the shadow of death. The time had come to climb the mountain of restoration. I had plenty of help, comfort, and support along the valley way. I had an abundance of gratitude for all of that support.

"Surely goodness and mercy shall follow me all the days of my life…"

Notwithstanding that support, it was clear to me I still had a very long way to go. I was determined but frightened at the same time.

As I headed up busy Interstate 45 toward Greenspoint, I tried to steady myself. *Don't be afraid, Cal, you can do this.* Cars whizzed by me. Those drivers were in the groove of rushing to work and running the expressway gauntlet. I'd forgotten all about that dynamic of daily work life. I tried hard to remember some of the other scriptures I had read and committed to memory over the years; passages dealing with overcoming fear, worry, and despair.

"For God hath not given us the spirit of fear; but of power, and of love, and of a sound mind". (I Timothy 1:7 KJV)

"These things I have spoken unto you, that in me ye might have peace. In the world ye shall have tribulation: but be of good cheer; I have overcome the world." (John 16:33 KJV)

When I pulled up to the call center building, I saw nothing had changed. The campus looked as beautiful as ever, and the parking lot was full; however, no welcoming committee or no fanfare greeted me. No fireworks or bombs went off. In fact, the morning started with a whimper. People were intently going about the business of working at a call center.

Lois greeted me with an embrace. I was overjoyed to see her again. My nerves calmed, and a sense of peace washed over me. There would be no infamy on this December morning.

"He leadeth me beside the still waters…"

She had a surprise for me. My office had been moved from the north side of the building near the busy call center floor to the secluded south side of the building. The new office had been previously used by a former senior executive vice president who had long since left the company. The huge corner office had large windows and beautiful cherry wood furniture. This space should have been reserved for Kathleen, whenever she chose to work at this campus. She had given it up for me, and Lois had prepared it for my return.

"He restoreth my soul..."

I immediately understood the plan. They moved me to a secluded part of the building to get me away from the staff. The thought of this didn't upset me at all. It made sense for several reasons. First of all, in this section, Lois sat right outside my door as opposed to across the building and separated by the front lobby. She became an official gatekeeper. No one could get in to see me without going through her. The other office left me open to unannounced visitors virtually all day. Having a gatekeeper made sense now. I appreciated the solitude of this office. It provided a haven in which to work on rebuilding confidence and comfort with my new persona. I checked e-mail and retrieved voice mail messages.

"He maketh me to lie down in green pastures..."

The doctors approved half days of work to enable me to test the waters. This was a good call on their part. By the time I got home in the early afternoon, I went right to bed in total exhaustion and didn't get up until the next morning. It wasn't the work so much as the drive and energy required to get out of bed and start the grind of getting ready for work. Once fully dressed and presentable, I then had to prepare myself mentally for the white-knuckled drive on the busy interstate system. Even though this commute took me away from downtown and against the majority of rush hour commuters, driving came awkwardly to me. I felt like a nervous wreck just as in years prior when I first learned to drive. By the time I reached the Greenspoint exit, my nerves were frazzled, and I felt spent.

I woke up the next morning with a long list of thoughts and questions about this job and my priorities in life. I couldn't help but ask myself a couple of questions over and over. *Still want to pursue being the top dog? How much does any of that matter now?* It hit me that I didn't care about being the top dog anymore. Oh, I would still enjoy the benefits of having a leadership role at a huge corporation, but the fire to move deftly past anything in my way to get to the very top had vanished. It only took one day back on the job to confirm that conclusion.

"I shall not want..."

Doc had called me her golden child. Where did that guy go? The title still fit, only his focus had shifted.

Things at work had kept on rolling without me. One of my colleagues had slid over from her duties to keep the call center going down the strategic path my team and I had decided to pursue. Was that a testament to my vision or her skill in leading and directing? Was it both? After all, her project management skill birthed the department in the first place. After some thought about this question, I took the credit, but the four-month walk I endured had changed my thinking completely. My conclusion wasn't born out of arrogance but another reason altogether. I decided things kept rolling because of my anointing for leadership. It had been ordained that I come to Houston to live and work at that contact center.

"Thou anointest my head with oil..."

Having an anointing bestowed upon your life results in big responsibilities. There are inherent principles that must be followed. The origin of anointing came from a practice of ancient shepherds. They poured oil on their sheep's heads. This act made it virtually impossible for insects to harm the sheep. This simple act became an object lesson in religious circles as anointing became symbolic of blessing, protection, and empowerment. Those with an anointing on their life are set apart for consecration, for officer duties, or religious service. In biblical times, people were anointed with oil to signify God's blessing. A person can be anointed for a special purpose: to be a king, to be a leader, or to be a builder. The leadership characteristic described me perfectly.

"The LORD is my shepherd..."

I believed that those anointed for the role of leadership have a responsibility to leave a legacy of greatness. The anointed one is to make sure the fruits and benefits of that anointing are passed along to the people they are exposed to; be they progeny, friends or fellow workers. I had done that. I had poured enough of myself out for my team to catch the vision of where we were going. This thing we begun, would continue for years to come.

"He leadeth me in the paths of righteousness..."

The measure of a leader's greatness is determined by how well that leader's followers carry on after the leader is gone. I had seen the anointing of leadership and service to others work time and time again. Price Love left a legacy for his boys and my mom. My dad and mom had taught me the lessons I needed to learn to be a father, a leader, and servant. I had saved enough money for my children to complete undergraduate study without accumulating crippling student loans. I had also passed along what I'd learned to my brother. Years later he would be in position to become the vice president of a huge corporation. He would finish the mountain climb I began. It was my job to point the way for those coming up behind me. An anointing comes with the responsibility of leaving a legacy of service, excellence, and success.

"I will dwell in the house of the LORD forever."

The December days passed, and I worked my half days in the peace and quietness of my anointing.

Chapter 19
MY OPTIONS

Making New Friends

AFTER SPENDING THE HOLIDAYS IN INDIANA, I flew back home to start my new life in earnest. The loneliness I experienced the previous summer rushed back upon me immediately. Only this time, it felt more intense. I wasn't all that confident about mingling or engaging in an active social life due to the aftereffects of Legionnaire's. I grew tired easily, and speaking in front of strangers embarrassed me into a torturing silence. Had it not been for Michele, I would have become a virtual recluse outside of work. She checked on me nearly every afternoon. Her tenderness and care for me chased the lonely blues away.

During that time, my young friend, Laura, introduced me to another potential set of friends. She had a couple of pets. Her cat demanded attention, but the pet that intrigued me was a really cool-looking fish.

"What...kind...of...fish...is ...th—th—that?" I had an extremely hard time saying words that began with "th" and "st."

"It's a betta, Cal. They are neat, especially the males. But you have to be careful, because they aren't very social. Like you." Laura giggled. "You don't need a fancy aquarium, because they can live in regular tap water. Just give them a decent-sized fish bowl and leave some room at the top so they can come up for air. You also have to leave room at the top when you fill the bowl, because they'll jump out if you fill it too full."

"No...way!" I had never heard of such a thing.

"It's true, man. These are great. Some people even have them on their desk at work."

The species was a beautiful Siamese fighting fish, more commonly known as a "betta." Male bettas hail from Southeast Asia and are especially colorful and exotic-looking with flowing and billowy fins. They don't tolerate other fish well and must be kept alone, because they have been known to kill other fish they believe are rivals. My curiosity about the three-year life expectancy of these small exotic fish drew me in. *Finally!* A friend that I could practice speaking to anytime I wanted, without worrying about him thinking I had a mental or hearing disability.

The next day, Laura and I were in the pet section of a discount store buying two male bettas. I picked up a couple medium-sized fish bowls and some betta fish food. I named the two bettas. "Option One" was a blue male and "Option Two," a maroon male. They both were stunning. Having two bettas gave me the choice of speaking to either one; thus the names Option One and Option Two. Once I got home, I placed them at opposite ends of a black table in my living room and moved the fern plants previously taking table space to my patio. I didn't want to place the bettas next to each other for fear they would try to jump into each other's bowls.

We were thick as thieves, me, my two Option boys, and the Brown Fellas. I fed Option One and Option Two and practiced my speech with them in the quiet of my living room. I talked to them about my days at work, Kristi and Geoffrey, and about anything else that came to mind. I kept a wary eye for Brown Fellas and became even more fanatical about keeping my flat spotless. The bettas were welcomed friends. Strange bacteria and tree roaches were not.

Michele would shake her head and laugh when I talked to the bettas. I came to rely on her probably much more than I should have. I had grown terribly fond of her and always wanted her around. The feeling was mutual, because when we were together, it was an all-out laugh fest. I needed all the levity I could get. I had found it.

She made sure I ate properly and cared for myself. She forced me out of the apartment and into the public eye. Michele watched me carefully and encouraged me to order for myself when we went to restaurants and push myself when I started to fade during outings. We rented movies, went window-shopping, and hung out. It was all clean fun. More often than not, I served as the butt of teasing.

"Come on, Handicap Man. Don't fade on me now. We've got twenty more stores to explore in this mall!" She'd squeeze my hand, and off we'd go to conquer more shops.

I learned to laugh at myself, thanks to my friend, and she inspired me to try to break out of my cocoon. I found myself growing more and more intrigued by her. Besides being fun-loving, she was straightforward. There were no mind games. If she thought something, she would share it, not rudely or with a calloused bluntness like mean-spirited people do sometimes. Her composition made her say, "I need to share exactly what's on my mind, so there is no misunderstanding about what I'm thinking or feeling." In a world where people don't always say what they mean, I found this straightforwardness refreshing. Ever since my August ordeal, I disliked playing mind games. Now, I preferred people be candid with me. I had learned life was too short for a bunch of foolishness.

Since we were work-out buddies before I got sick, she encouraged me to stop lying around home in the afternoon. I would meet her at the fitness club to lift weights and to do light work-outs. When it came to workouts, all the jokes and fun stopped. My funny friend turned into a drill sergeant.

My rail-thin muscles couldn't lift much weight. She put me to shame. Her weight workouts were intense, and she didn't treat me with kid gloves during the various exercises. Early on, when we were doing chest and biceps exercises, I only lifted the bar as opposed to a set of weights. My sense of coordination and balance continued to be very poor, thanks to lingering ataxia. I couldn't lift the bar and hold it level at the same time. The mighty had fallen.

"Come on, Cal, hold it straight." Her voice was firm and direct. One of the professional trainers at the club, Kimberly, watched intently. She shook her head in disagreement a couple times.

The pity I'd come to expect from any interaction with people didn't show with Michele. She pushed me to keep moving along the path of recovery and told me I'd have to "buck up" if I wanted to get strong again. I had a hard time keeping up. I didn't want her to know this failure depressed me. Seeds of self-doubt crept into my mind. I had rarely failed at anything during my life.

One evening, we stopped at a fast-food joint and got burgers and fries to take back to my place. This served as a reward after several days of good nutrition and solid workouts. I ate soft food for the most part and had not really tried eating burgers yet. I took a big bite of my burger and coughed violently. I was embarrassed and disappointed all at once. I wanted desperately to be "normal" in every aspect, but it wouldn't happen this night. I couldn't even eat a cheeseburger without nearly choking to death.

Before I knew it, I began to sob. Instead of the obligatory long hug and comforting, she put her hand on my shoulder and challenged me to work on chewing slowly and concentrating. Vintage Michele tough-love came through. It's what I really needed at that moment instead of a companion at a pity party. She would help me. She wouldn't let me play the invalid card around her. This episode changed the way I thought about how I wanted people to treat me from that point on. That moment taught me that I didn't really want pity about my new persona. Support, yes; pity, no. I had to learn how to deal with my disability and live my life to the fullest in spite of it. Once I stopped crying, in normal Michele style, she cracked a quick-witted joke, and we both giggled. She always had a way of teasing me and taking the edge off at the right time.

"At least you're cute!" That statement, coupled with crossed eyes and a tongue stuck out in my direction, led to a soft kiss to finish the job.

My giggle turned into laughter, and I broke through the tears. Instead of continued choking, I started a protracted belly laugh. I felt alive and never better.

After she left, I told the betta boys all about the cheeseburger ordeal. They swam around and ignored me completely.

"No...res...pect! I...am...the...person...fee...ding...you...boys." No mercy. They were just like Michele: aloof to my pity parties.

Her view of my motor skills applied not only to weightlifting and eating but my driving as well. I tried to drive us around for each excursion. I scared years off the life of my poor girlfriend. She put a stop to being chauffeured soon after the venturing out began.

"Dude, I'm driving. You are way too skittish. You're bucking me around like a bronco, man."

My driving was indeed horrific. I braked incessantly and oversteered. Driving in and around Rice Village challenged me because of heavy traffic due to the area's popularity. My freeway driving pushed her over the edge. It compared to an adventure that would have struck fear into the heart of Indiana Jones.

The tough love thing made me concentrate and become more determined to regain my running prowess. I worked really hard at keeping my balance and controlling my gait during morning runs. As a result, my running got better. I could run nearly five miles now. The Legionnaire's disease had diminished my lung capacity. I tired more easily than ever before, and I couldn't seem to reach top speed anymore. I would get confirmation of that by the end of the month.

The bulletin board at the fitness club had a poster announcing a five-kilometer race. The race was scheduled for Saturday, January 27, 2001. This would be my first race since being stricken with Legionnaire's disease. I couldn't think of a better scenario: 3.1-mile race with the start and finish at the Museum of Art in Houston's museum district no more than a mile and a half from my apartment.

When the big day came, the excitement made it hard to contain myself. I got up early to eat a couple of bananas and make sure I properly hydrated. The sun shined brightly, and the temperature measured in the low sixties. Runners had been given a perfect morning for running a 5K. I thought about all the duels I had with Team Fudd. I couldn't beat the Beasleys or Ward, but I could pretty much count on outkicking everyone else at that short distance. Diller always hung right with me and would press all the way to the end. I had him to thank for finishing well under seventeen minutes more than once.

Should I run down to the start, or should I drive? If I ran down to the start, it might hurt my chances of doing a fast time, because I'd already be tired. I nervously pondered this decision for nearly a half hour before pushing myself into my SUV then driving a mile down the West U side streets to get close to the start.

Once I found a place to park, I got on my racing shoes and made sure my bib number, 3069, fit properly on my singlet with safety pins. After a few stretching exercises, I started on my way, jogging toward the start line. I picked up speed to loosen my muscles. I felt as light as a feather. The feeling of butterflies I had experienced so many times before other races came rushing back. It all seemed so familiar and comfortable.

Before I knew it, the gun fired, and we were on our way. Instead of bolting out and running a fast first mile as I used to do, I found myself running a very pedestrian pace just under seven minutes per mile. Funny thing is, I worked very hard, and it felt as though I had reached top speed. Things weren't quite the same. I couldn't motor and run away from the pack. Suddenly, I realized it really didn't matter. A radiant smile spread across my face. I kept looking up at the blue sky. A feeling of euphoria and ecstasy washed over me. I began to praise God in my thoughts as I ran. *Thank you, Lord, for raising me up from my death bed and letting me live.*

The second and third miles were the same. A feeling of overwhelming joy flooded my body. I was in tune with everything around me including the race fans, beautiful homes sporting well-manicured lawns, and fresh air. I felt as one with the world. Before I knew it, I neared the finish and a throng of cheering spectators. Suddenly, I came crashing back to earth. My lungs were seared. I spotted the finish clock and saw the seconds ticking past the nineteen-minute mark. *Wow, was I this slow now?* I tried to sprint to finish under twenty minutes. I just made it. I wasn't among the top finishers, but I had finished. When I got clear of the finish chute, I kneeled down and kissed the ground. *I did it. Hallelujah!!*

I couldn't wait to get home to tell Option One and Option Two all about the race and show them the official black race t-shirt with the fancy Fine Arts logo.

As I walked into my apartment, I found Option Two lying lifeless on the floor, in colorful contrast to the light brown carpet of my living room floor. He had leapt out of his bowl for freedom or to attack someone or something and met an untimely death instead. Tears streamed down my face as I gently touched him and then wrapped him in tissue paper.

It made for a bittersweet morning, but by evening, I had made another trip to the discount store to get a replacement betta. This new beautiful turquoise male would do fine. Welcome home Option Three!

I would have to be very careful about not overfilling the fishbowls and make sure I had fresh water. Later that morning, I walked to Kroger to buy a couple gallons of distilled water for the next filling in a week or so. My Options deserved the best.

The days after that first race were filled with work and continuing the quest to get back in shape. Michele introduced me to Kimberly, the trainer who had been watching us work out together. Michele had explained my ordeal to Kimberly who had then taken it upon herself to study Legionnaire's disease and the effects of ataxia. She had developed a special exercise routine for me. The workouts Kimberly selected centered on activities that would improve balance and core strength. It's just what I needed. I began to meet with her two or three times a week. Now I could work out with Kim or Michele. This arrangement suited me as I found other activities to share with Michele. Dating her proved easier and more fun than working out with her.

Kim stressed the importance of taking it easy and focusing on a few things at a time. No need to pressure myself or push for speedy results. She patiently supported me, not out of pity but simply out of the desire to train me properly. She believed in the importance of paying attention to details and pacing oneself during the various exercises.

I should have learned that lesson in caring for Option One and Option Three. Instead of changing their fish bowls using tap water as Laura told me to do, I used the distilled water I bought at Kroger. I wasn't quite sure if ignoring this detail was a mistake with fatal consequences for the Options. After a few days, both boys started looking sick and moving slowly.

Option One went first. He floated to the top of his bowl and gulped his last. Option Three lasted a few days longer, but he met a similar fate. Who would I practice my speech on now? What happened? It might have been the distilled water. What a dummy. Laura had told me to use tap water, and I'd let that go right over my head. Had I murdered my friends because I listened poorly? It's another thing I had to change in my life. I had to listen more carefully.

Option Four, another maroon male, became my answer and final attempt to make the betta experiment work. It did. I kept him for months and months. I even took him to work and put him on my desk. He made for great conversation. He was so beautiful and exotic. People would laugh when I shared his name.

"Option Four? What a funny name. Why did you name him that?"

"Uh...Op...tions...One...Two...and...Th—Th—Three...died." A big shoulder shrug and grin from me always prompted a return smile or giggle. I've always liked making people smile.

Chapter 20
"This Call May Be
Taped or Monitored."

A New Treasured Possession and Dealing with "the Look"

Nearly every company with any meaningful customer base had a call center by Y2K. Some had outsourced their call center operations to India or the Philippines. Some employed domestic centralized or multiple regional centers. Still others had a wide web of home-based customer service representatives handling calls 24/7, 365 days a year. No matter which type of call center a consumer calls, it is likely he will hear the familiar phrase along the lines of: "For quality assurance purposes, this call may be taped or monitored."

Call center managers love call monitoring and recording technology. They use it for training, snooping on customer service representatives, complaint review, and quality assurance. Although the phrase is almost a cliché, it's not a joke. Calls really are monitored and many are recorded. In fact, in the financial services industry, virtually every call is recorded. These recordings protect both the investor and the financial institution when money is moved from one account to another or securities are traded.

Most call centers have a specially trained staff to monitor phone representatives and provide feedback and coaching. CSRs are trained to listen carefully for opportunities to expand a company's wallet share with each customer, be empathetic, and provide excellent service. The quality assurance professionals make sure that happens. They do this job primarily by randomly selecting call recordings, employing a scoring scheme, and then sharing the results with managers and CSRs. Another technique quality assurance professionals use from time to time is role playing during training or coaching sessions.

In June 2000, I decided it would be a good idea to go through quality assurance training with a group of CSRs in my call center. The trainer made the exercise fast-paced and fun. During the course of the two-day session, every participant performed a customer service role play with a partner. These role plays were recorded on cassette tape and then played to the entire class for critique and feedback.

My partner Jason and I were asked to pretend we were a dry cleaning customer and counter worker engaged in a telephone conversation. I played the role of the counter worker, while Jason posed as a potential customer calling to check out services and prices. I spoke smoothly and pleasantly making sure I followed the protocol established by the quality assurance professional running the class. Our call went well. We each received our very own recording of the call as a keepsake.

Now Option Four wasn't the only conversation piece on my desk. The other took the form of this cassette tape. It had become my prized possession. It contained the only recording I owned of my speaking voice before being afflicted with dysarthria. I had rediscovered it buried with some other keepsake items after I returned to work. During 2001, I listened to it nearly every day. Playing it became a new ritual.

There were two reasons why I played the tape almost every day. The first reason was simply to practice speaking by imitating my own voice. I listened to portions of the tape and then repeated phrases trying to mimic my old enunciation, cadence, and intonation. I worked particularly hard on words starting with "s," "t," and "th" because of difficulty pronouncing them. I also kept a list of words I had difficulty saying on a pocket-sized notepad. I would listen for those words on the tape and try to emulate them. I served as my own personal quality assurance professional. Sometimes I would give myself a good grade. Other times, I would be weepy and sorry for myself when I wasn't even close to speaking exactly like the voice on the cassette tape.

I also played the tape for people who met me after August 2000 so they would see how I used to speak. There were some deep-rooted thoughts going on in my mind about this process. Some days, I still had a deep conflict about my persona. Was I the well-spoken guy on the tape who wanted to rule the world? Or was I the new guy learning to get comfortable with disability and just glad to be alive? In many ways, I wanted to identify with the person role playing with Jason in terms of speaking ability, but I tried really hard to be happy with myself— Legionnaire's warts and all.

Normally, I'd tell the story about my compelling Legionnaire's survival experience and then I'd pull out the cassette.

"Hold…on…I…want…you…to…hear…some…thing."

I would retrieve an old-school black and silver cassette tape player from the credenza in my office, plug it into an outlet, and place it on my desk. After some minor fussing and adjustments, I would press play. Jason and I stepped through our exercise, voices clear and strong.

At the conclusion, I always asked the same question: "Do.. ...you... know...who... th—that.. ...was?"

Sometimes a listener would guess the voice belonged to me, but most often, they wouldn't. More often than not, people would be surprised or shocked at the voice on the tape. The dysarthria had completely changed the tone, cadence, and delivery of my speaking voice.

There were other times I wished I could produce the tape and play it for an audience. In these instances, playing the tape would help prevent "the Look." I wanted to play the tape at rental-car counters, restaurants, checkout counters, and any other place where I opened my mouth to speak in a public exchange. Many times "the Look" (the frowns and stares that said, "What's wrong with this guy?") broke my heart. I wanted to tell them, *I am a vice president at a huge corporation managing a department with 250 employees reporting to me.* Dr. Kevorkian's words always came back to me in those instances: "People are mean, and it will be very hard." Strangers wouldn't care about me being a corporate star or quick witted. All they could see was a frail-looking black man who mumbled unintelligibly. If I could only play the tape, people wouldn't think I was mentally challenged or hearing impaired. I wouldn't see the Look. They would know a brilliant man simply trapped in a Legionnaire's-ravaged body stood before them.

I had to figure out a way to turn these interactions in my favor. To prevent this horrible feeling, sometimes I would play a game when I got the Look that precluded the need for playing the cassette tape. Occasionally, a person working a counter or serving me would assume I was deaf. The mischievous Calvin would show up. I would point to my ears, shake my head, and then utter a disarming phrase.

"I...can...read...your...lips." It wasn't a lie. I could read their lips. They just didn't know I could hear their voices as well. I overemphasized my trouble saying the words for effect and laughed to myself. Invariably, the person would be comfortable with that mode of communication and smile, eyes gleaming. The next few words from them would be warm and measured to make sure I could "read" every one. I nodded my head in affirmation and smiled. For the moment, I became a normal "deaf" person instead of a freak show.

It had been fun playing this game. My friends and family would laugh when I told the stories of faking it. But it also taught me a lesson. I could never again flash the Look myself. No more insensitive thoughts about a person with a disability or with attributes or beliefs different from my own. How many times had I heard "Never judge a book by its cover"? Now I knew exactly what that saying meant.

I would keep the cassette tape within reach and play it periodically for years to come, even as my speaking began to improve, and I could speak nearly as fast as I could think. Old habits die hard. Call center managers retain some recordings for a very long time to substantiate facts. This recording fell into that category.

Chapter 21

"NAWLINS"

Reunited with the Fudds!

WITH THE THE FIRST 5K BEHIND me, I could begin to concentrate on my next big physical challenge of running the upcoming Mardi Gras Half Marathon in New Orleans. During the mid-1990s, the Tri-Fudds started a tradition of traveling to New Orleans to run the annual Mardi Gras Marathon. This race was unlike any other in the country. In true New Orleans style, it featured a party atmosphere and a real celebration of Mardi Gras. As such, participants were encouraged to run in costumes. In the 1999 event, two of the Tri-Fudds, Jon and Kirk, dressed as French maids. They looked hilarious. I can't imagine how they ran 26.2 miles dressed in little black dresses, laced aprons, fishnet hosiery, big hair wigs, full make-up, and funniest of all, humongous fake breasts. All this after we all had a long night of swilling beer, drinking hurricanes, and going from club to club to dance and listen to music. They got catcalls during the whole race and won an award from the race sponsors for having one of the best costumes.

We made going to New Orleans a big deal. Jon and Scott hosted Mardi Gras parties and encouraged everyone on Team Fudd to make the trip to "Nawlins." That 1999 trip meant fun for me, too, because Rod went with me. He never competed as a serious runner or cyclist, but the trip provided the opportunity for us to hang out with the Fudd boys, relax, and have fun. His college roommate, and our Alpha Phi Alpha fraternity brother, Gerald, lived in New Orleans. Seeing Gerald represented a special treat for Rod to see his pledge brother.

Gerald helped us navigate Bourbon Street and the rest of the French Quarter. Since he worked for the city of New Orleans, he gave us some unique perspectives about the history and culture of the city. He also shared another fact with us that made us behave. As we walked down Bourbon Street, Gerald carefully pointed out cameras mounted in various positions on the buildings. Cameras were all over the place!

"Man, these women come down here lifting their shirts for beads. They don't even know it's all on tape. You're likely to see anything up on the balconies."

Later that evening, I believed him. As we walked up and down Bourbon Street, in the darkness and cover of night, women bared their naked breasts to onlookers. This prompted the men standing above the street on balconies to toss necklaces made of colorful beads down to them as a reward for the show. All the pretty women who exposed themselves had more necklaces than one could count. My eyes bulged, and my mouth gaped in naiveté. I had never experienced anything like this in my small town. The show didn't stop there. I saw a completely nude woman being fondled by a man right in the open on one of the balconies above Bourbon Street. My jaw dropped. I almost knocked Rod and the rest of the guys over trying to get their attention to look up.

I elbowed Rod repeatedly. "Man, did you see that?" Our heads were on a swivel taking in all the sites. Somewhere a guy watching videotape of all this must be enjoying himself.

I had skipped the 2000 Team Fudd annual Nawlins adventure because of moving to Houston in February and starting a new job. I eagerly anticipated getting back there to hang out with my friends. More importantly, this would be a huge test of my resolve and my body's ability. Finishing the race after all I'd been through would be a miracle.

Jogging to prepare for a 5K differed vastly from preparing for a half or full marathon. In the past, I had the help of Team Fudd to train and prepare for long grueling runs. Over the years, the long distances were always difficult for me. Although I had run a couple strong half marathons, I thought about all the failed attempts to qualify for the Boston marathon. I remembered Yoder blowing by me at the ten-mile mark of a half marathon several years ago. Now, I didn't have the luxury of my Team Fudd support group.

Working on cardio training alone in Houston had been tough. I had sorely missed the camaraderie of my longtime training buddies. In addition, I had become very discouraged about not being able to run at top speed anymore. My fitness trainer, Kimberly, helped solve that problem. As she trained me in the club, she introduced me to Kevin. He would provide the male training bonding I had missed since leaving Team Fudd behind. Kevin also worked for my company.

"What's up, man? I see you've been working out with Kim. That's good."

"Yep...she...is...help...ing. ...me...with ...th...bal...ance...and...st—st—st—strength."

"She told me what happened to you. You're doing really well. I heard you were really cut before."

"Yeah." I wondered who told him that. I had rarely been in the club before getting Legionnaire's disease. Most of the time, I did cardio training alone in the early morning darkness. I never thought of myself as "cut." I certainly wasn't "cut" now.

"You can get it back. Have you been back on your bike yet?"

Good question. I had been to Rice to ride a couple times, but I wasn't happy with the results. I couldn't ride fast, and I couldn't stand up and pedal anymore. I found myself super nervous when riding now. Balancing the bike didn't come easy. I hadn't ventured out to the countryside yet. I really didn't want to get into all that with this guy.

"Uh-uh."

"We should go riding sometimes. We could get some runs in, too!"

"Okay. I...want...to...bench...press...like...you. Man... you...are... st—st—strong!" I hated stuttering.

He flexed his biceps and flashed a confident grin. "You can do this, Cal."

I went back to my program with Kimberly, but inside I bubbled. It would be great to work out with someone else who seemed pretty serious. Kevin was a monster with the weights. He bench-pressed darn near every weight in the gym. I'd seen him leave the club to run outside on the bayou. That let me know he believed in total fitness.

I had worked myself up to a five-mile run a couple weeks before the Mardi Gras half marathon. That would have to carry me through. I looked forward to training runs with Kevin. I thought seriously about taking him up on the offer of going on short bike rides together. Hopefully, the rides wouldn't be too intense. I wanted to make them just challenging enough for me to start to regain some confidence. He had told me about another event I would think about after the half marathon. It was a 175-mile, two-day ride from Houston to Austin in April. My whole body tingled with excitement. Could I push myself to do that now? *Slow down, big boy. One thing at a time.*

This year, I wouldn't be flying from Indiana with the rest of the guys. I would be driving from Houston. So I had two big challenges: first, building a training regimen that would prepare me to run 13.1 miles. I thought nervously about the skimpy amount of training I had done so far, but I believed I could finish the race if I took my time and didn't press. If I couldn't do anything about improving my speech, I would do everything in my power to return to an active athletic life. The second challenge was making the five-hour drive to New Orleans.

The second challenge ended up being a pleasant surprise. I had always been a good highway driver. I especially liked driving at night during long trips. In fact, I loved it because of the lighter traffic. I could be alone with my thoughts accompanied only by background music. The natural feeling of highway driving came back as soon as I cleared the Houston city limits headed east on Interstate 10. It was virtually a straight shot down I-10 all the way to New Orleans. There were no passengers. It was just me, my car, and comforting music.

The drive took me across southeast Texas into Louisiana through Lake Charles to Lafayette. From Lafayette, I encountered some of the most scenic highway driving I had ever seen. The highway crossed the largest swamp in the United States, the Atchafalaya Swamp. The eighteen-mile bridge across the swamp is on elevated pillars and presented breathtaking views of the Atchafalaya River, bayous, bald cypress swamps, and marshes. I couldn't help but be thankful that I had lived to see this beautiful vista. My eyes drank in the green splendor, and my mind thought about the magnificence of my God who created all this.

It got better. Once I passed the swamp, I continued east toward Baton Rouge across the mighty Mississippi River. The majestic Mississippi held some significance for me and my family. I marveled at its power as I drove over it.

The memories came flooding back as strong as the mighty river itself. When I worked for LNIMC, one of my trips led me to Memphis on the banks of the great river to look at real estate. I would eventually finance a luxury apartment complex in a prominent Memphis suburb. Closing that deal meant a proud accomplishment for me. I had completed a multimillion dollar investment roughly fifty miles from the birthplace of my parents, who had grown up as poor sharecroppers.

During the due diligence visit, our mortgage bankers in Memphis took me south to the river boat casinos across the Tennessee state line to Tunica, Mississippi. I called my Mom to tell her I was in the vicinity of her beloved Frenchmans Bayou. She giggled.

"Oh, I wish I was there, CK. You remember the stories I told you about Tunica?"

"Of course I do, Doc! I know my history." Doc had shared stories about my Mama Lucy's father, my great-grandfather, getting into trouble with the law in Tunica. After his crime, he hid in a levee for days and crossed the Mississippi River under the cover of night into Arkansas to the safety of relatives.

"Good. I love Memphis and Tunica. We should all take a trip there so we can visit Frenchmans Bayou."

"It's a great idea, Doc. We should do that."

I was overjoyed to see the old gang as well as the Beasley's parents, Jack and June. We all enjoyed the perfect New Orleans sunny, cool, and dry weather. Jon and Scott's sister, Brenda, and I lived in Texas, so we were used to that. Everyone else had flown down from Indiana and was still dealing with ice and snow at home.

While we enjoyed a nice dinner and walked the French Quarter, this year the partying and merry-making wasn't as intense as my last trip to New Orleans a couple years before. After a short while of reveling, I tired and wanted to get back to the hotel to rest for the next morning.

The day of reckoning had come; February 4, 2001, the thirty-sixth Mardi Gras Marathon. There were actually three races: a 5K, the half marathon, and a full marathon. The races drew about 4,750 runners (including about 2,300 in the marathon), the most ever. There were about 1,600 runners registered for the half marathon.

Brian and I lined up together at the start. He planned to run the full marathon but had agreed to stay with me for a while. That was a huge sacrifice. He should have stayed back to run a slower pace to position himself to finish the grueling 26.2 miles. The gesture served as a testament to our friendship. I remembered the October night he cried at my house because he thought I didn't have long to live. But here we were together, at the start line, on a crisp sunny New Orleans morning four months later to test our bodies in ways few people ever do.

We stretched and tried to keep things light. The start of a marathon is awe inspiring. People of all shapes and colors have sacrificed many hours and run countless miles to prepare for an unbelievable test of mind and body. Normally, runners cram close together to get as near the start line as possible. It is an elbow-to-elbow crush of humanity with a pronounced smell of ointment to soothe muscles. The positive vibe engulfing those at the start elicits all kinds of emotions. People around us were laughing, joking, and cheering. Others were stoic and focused. I was a bundle of nerves, but I couldn't stop giggling thanks to Brian's quips.

People run marathons for all sorts of reasons. I had mine. If I could pull this off, I would show everyone God's miracle healing power. I would also prove that I had uncommon drive and determination. It would be an example for others to follow, to take note of, and to share. It represented personal freedom. I had a disability, but I could go anywhere and do anything. I wouldn't be limited or relegated to a life of pity and inaction. I had become a winner again.

As the gun sounded and we ran the early miles, the same sense of joy and euphoria I experienced the week before during my first race returned. Running through the streets of New Orleans was a special treat. The city was beautiful, and the spectators were loud. The cheers and Brian's encouragement powered me through the first eight miles. I found myself waving and smiling at the crowds.

Just after mile eight, we approached a steep bridge. I began to get a cramp in my side, and I stumbled.

"You okay?" Brian asked.

"My...si—side." I could hardly speak. I grabbed my torso. I had entered no-man's land of running miles farther than I had trained in over seven months. It made sense that my body would start to let me know I had entered a zone I hadn't visited in an awfully long time. Even though I was only running just under eight minutes per mile, my lungs were beginning to yell for air. This feeling was completely foreign. I had grown accustomed to easily running half marathons at seven minutes each mile. Those days were long gone.

Brian touched my arm, and we paused for just a few seconds. "You can do it, Cal. Just relax, and let's get over this hill."

It worked. We powered our way up the bridge one step at a time. Brian shouted encouragement every few steps. Before I knew it, we were at mile twelve with a little over a mile to go. There was no way I'd let myself blow up as I did at mile ten some fifteen years earlier in Indiana. I looked over at Brian and grabbed his hand with a huge smile on my face.

"Th—th—th—thanks...I'm...go...ing."

He waved me on. I ran as hard as I could to the finish inside the Superdome. I crossed the finish line and pumped my fists in the air. I was skinny and frail, but I had finished a half marathon in one hour and forty-two minutes, only five months after nearly dying from Legionnaire's disease. This personal triumph could be shared with my family and friends. I ordered a poster-size picture of myself crossing the finish line with skinny arms raised above my head.

I had finished 173rd out of 1,600 half marathon participants. Once I caught my breath, I collected myself and ate several cups of jambalaya and drank water and Gatorade in the runner's refreshment area. I waited for my friends to finish the marathon by taking in the sights and sounds of other runners congregating after the race. It was a good day for the Tri-Fudds. We were all winners. Brian finished his marathon, powered by a strong half marathon playing wingman to his friend, Cal. Team Fudd had conquered "Nawlins" once again.

Chapter 22
MANY RETURNS

Visiting the Cradle of My Family

IT WAS APRIL FOOL'S DAY, BUT this wasn't a joke. I rented a car and drove from Houston to Fort Wayne. Driving to New Orleans had given me the confidence to take another huge step in staking my independence. I had asked for vacation days because this week would be big. My siblings and I were hosting a retirement and birthday party for Doc. She would soon turn sixty-two and had decided to retire from the Fort Wayne State Hospital. She had been employed there, on and off, for over thirty years. She loved taking care of the patients. I had a hard time believing she would actually go through with this.

We planned a banquet dinner and invited all of Doc's friends, co-workers, and family. They came. We were especially pleased to see her brothers, Joe and Ted. This became a family reunion in my mom's honor. She deserved this. My sister Linda ordered a limousine to pick her up and drive her to the party. We had a red carpet leading from the parking area to the entrance of the venue. Everyone enjoyed a feast. Flowers adorned the place. I counted thirteen dozen roses behind the podium where person after person stood to pay tribute to Doc's many years of service. The speeches were a true testament to a life that mattered and made a difference in the lives of people who couldn't help themselves.

When she found out I planned to drive to Ft. Wayne for the celebration, she had a fit. Her faith never wavered as I went through the darkest days, but she grew very concerned about my health and well being as the days unfolded. She thought a thousand-plus-mile drive across the country didn't make sense and would be too much for me to handle.

I had told her the stories of "the Look." She always worried about me whenever I made trips between Indiana and Texas. Seeing me in action gave her further reason for pause. I still drank only with the help of a straw, I choked when I ate, my memory was spotty, and there were times in which my brain seemed scrambled to her. I still had a very difficult time stringing together sentences and communicating effectively. She feared I would have trouble on the highway and would be taken advantage of or harmed, especially in the Deep South. I thought her concern was overblown, but I had fostered the problem.

I fought terrible depression and had confided in Doc about it. She'd seen me sobbing on the weekends I flew to Indiana to see Geoff and Kris. I didn't think things were going well with them at all. They were hurt and disappointed with me for not moving back home for good after getting sick. On top of that, I poured out my soul to Doc about struggles at work, money issues, and the arguments with Bernice about my leaving her. I also discussed disappointment with my physical condition and the loneliness of living in Houston so far away from all my loved ones. Ever the woman of faith, she prayed for me and encouraged me best she could. I began to think I needed to talk to a professional about all this but tucked those thoughts away. After all, I wasn't crazy, just terribly sad.

This presented an interesting paradox, because I had made the conversion from working half days to full-time just a couple weeks before I left for the retirement party. It had almost been a nonevent. As the December days turned to spring 2001, I got more and more comfortable making the commute to work and then spending the morning hours in my office. I found myself frequently working past noon. It wasn't a big deal. The directors kept things going, and we were embarking on some key initiatives. We were also continuing our quest to raise the level of talent in our call center. Things were going well.

For the most part, we were hitting our service goals. Kathleen provided her support and patience. She still drove for results, but she did so in fairness. I couldn't ask for much more than that. Earlier in the month, she had a strategic planning meeting in which all her direct reports had to provide an update of our departments. The meeting lasted all day long in a conference room overlooking lush green grounds and a picturesque greenway.

As we met that day, like every other day, runners, bikers, and walkers zipped by on the greenway. I would sneak peeks whenever I could and wish I was outside instead of at a strategic planning meeting. Things had changed for me. In the past, I would have been so dialed in, I would have hardly noticed outside distractions. Now, virtually all I could think about was grabbing my running shoes after the meeting and getting outside for a run.

The room was set up with tables in a huge U-shape so we could see each other. This setting required me to focus, overcome fatigue, and present. One by one, each participant gave their PowerPoint presentations. I was one of the last directors to present. I passed around my presentation copies and began to slowly and deliberately tell the story of the call center. My teeth were chattering and underneath the table my legs and feet wiggled wildly.

My counterparts nodded and shook their heads in affirmation. They seemed to hang on to every syllable. I spoke literally one syllable at a time. When I finished, I got an ovation. Dr. K may have been wrong. Everyone wasn't mean. This wasn't my family, but they cared about me and made allowances. They made my return to full-time work triumphant.

As I left Houston on April Fool's Day, I took the same route I took to New Orleans a month before. I drove back through Louisiana over the breathtaking Atchafalaya Swamp and the bridge across the mighty Mississippi River and through Baton Rouge. Instead of turning south toward New Orleans, I headed northeast through Mississippi to Memphis where I would spend the night.

As I drove past Natchez, Mississippi, I decided to call Doc to let her know I was on my way. "Guess...wh—where...I...am...Doc?"

"Where, baby?"

"Nat...chez."

"Natchez? What in the world are you doing in Natchez?"

"Dri...ving...th—th—through...on...my...way...up...th—th—there."

"Oh my God, CK, you shouldn't be driving this far. It's dangerous." She had experienced my new style of driving but was concerned for another reason. Growing up in the South had provided memories of blacks being mistreated, especially when they stopped in small towns. I wasn't concerned. This was the New Millennium. I had heard there was a new South.

"Doc...don't...wor...ry...I'll...be...fine. See...you...to...mor...row."

"Be careful. Stop and rest, but be careful where you stop."

"Doc...bye!"

I wasn't going to let her pass along a negative vibe. I had to do this. Besides, I had a grand idea. The trip would take me into northwestern Arkansas right past Turrell, Frenchmans Bayou, and Joiner. I planned to stop to look around and take pictures. I could hardly sleep that night at the hotel in West Memphis. I lay awake watching for bacteria and trying to figure out the plan for the return to the birthplace of my parents.

The people at the front desk had never heard of Frenchmans Bayou even though it was only thirty miles away. Not a good start. Thank goodness the gas station next door sold maps of Arkansas. I spotted my target on Highway 61. Frenchmans Bayou appeared as one of those towns labeled with a very small circle on a map. The name was much bigger than the circle. At least it showed up on the map!

I drove north up Interstate 55 looking for the Frenchmans Bayou exit. I drove and drove and drove. Soon, I approached Osceola, almost fifty miles north of Memphis. Had I passed the Frenchmans Bayou exit? I pulled off at a rest stop to look at the map posted in the pavilion. I found the town on a huge wall map, but there was no exit off I-55. I'd have to exit at Osceola and drive east to state road 61 and then due south to the towns I wanted to visit.

My palms were sweating, and my heart pounded as I drove south down state road 61. The early blues bands traveled this highway. Doc had told me stories of B. B. King passing through the region playing clubs up and down the 61 corridor. I imagined Price Love driving this very highway doing business. What would I find? After twenty minutes, I came upon Joiner.

I hadn't been to Joiner in thirty-five years. My parents had taken me and Linda with them there to visit their best friends, Frank and Claudia and their three boys. I couldn't remember where they lived or much about this town at all except playing baseball with the boys and getting hit in the face with a baseball bat. I ran to Mom for comforting. Frank and Claudia's boys snickered and teased me when I came back outside to finish the game. I just couldn't remember anything else about this place. So after a few short minutes, I drove the five miles to Frenchmans Bayou.

My heart rate sped up again, and I had trouble holding my hands steady on the steering wheel. A million thoughts raced through my mind. What would I find? Who would I see? Finally, the town unfolded before my eyes. I stopped at the city limits to take a picture of the welcome sign. The sign contained several bullet holes, and the area was overgrown with weeds and littered with trash. This classic small, country town had passed its prime. There were a couple abandoned buildings in town and not much else. I drove the area and took pictures of the train tracks, street signs, and the river where my mom was baptized near a small Baptist church.

I couldn't find any evidence of the businesses my grandfather owned. My guess was all the buildings had long since disappeared. The town was completely deserted except for a spanking new post office. I pulled into the parking lot and went inside. A middle-aged white woman behind the counter greeted me with a warm smile.

"Hello. Can I help you, young man?"

"I'm...just...pass...ing...th—th—through...town. My...mo...ther... was...born...here. It...is...a...love...ly...town." I lied. It was desolate and ugly.

"Well, thank you." She didn't give me "the Look." Her face was pleasant and relaxed.

"My...grand...fa...th—ther...Price...Love...and...my...fam...i...ly... lived...near...and...worked...for...the...Speck...fami ...ly."

"Well, my last name is Speck."

Her face beamed. She mentioned her husband's name and pointed in the direction of their home. The man knew my grandfather. His father did business with Price Love many years before. This conversation made all the stories Doc told me become real. Suddenly, this abandoned town had life.

"Do...you...th—th—think...I...could...get...a...pos...t...st—st—stamp...of...French...mans...Ba...you?"

"Why, sure you can. Let's see if I can find a piece of paper." She retrieved several blank sheets of paper and affixed the Frenchmans Bayou postal stamps on each. It was April 2, 2001—my sister Carla's thirty-seventh birthday. Doc's beloved Frenchmans Bayou had become mine too. I'd returned to my roots.

By the end of the week in Ft. Wayne, I had the pictures I'd taken enlarged and framed. I also framed the sheet of paper which contained the postal stamp. They still adorn the walls of Mom's dining room to this day. I presented them to Doc at her retirement party. As I did, I teased her and my uncle Joe and Ted.

"French...mans...Bay...ou. The...town...with...a...new...post...off...ice...but...no...people." The crowd laughed, and so did I.

Chapter 23
THE "TRIFECTA"

Inspired to Overcome the Ultimate Physical Challenge

SOME PEOPLE JUST HAVE NATURAL ATHLETIC ability. They can run faster, jump higher, and move more quickly than others. I knew my son Geoffrey had these qualities early on. He had "it." He wasn't the first in my family with athletic talent. I wasn't an all-star, but I wasn't a couch potato either. Pops starred as a basketball player at Turrell High School in Arkansas back in the 1950s, but the real athletic ability rested in Doc's genes.

Her baby brother, Emmitt "Charles" Love, became a legitimate high school basketball star at Austin High School in Chicago and eventually wound up with a scholarship to play Division I basketball at Nebraska University. His brash, confident style and his game fit the mold you would expect from a guy who hailed from Chicago's tough West Side.

Doc had even more impressive athletic connections. Her first cousins were all-star athletes in the late 1960s and early 1970s. Alex Johnson starred as an outfielder and designated hitter for thirteen seasons with several major league baseball teams. While Alex excelled in Major League Baseball, his brother Ron made a name for himself as a standout running back at the University of Michigan and as an MVP-caliber running back in the NFL. Ron and Alex were the pride of our family during my boyhood years.

Like his relatives, Geoffrey would eventually ride his God-given athletic ability to bigger things. He was the sports star every dad wants. I saw myself living vicariously through his accomplishments. The talent began to show itself while, as a young boy, he tried to slam dunk on a miniature basketball hoop in our basement with his best friend, AJ. I had never been around a more competitive child. He loved sports and absolutely hated to lose. The thought of losing at anything drove him to tears. This is a trait he inherited from me. I hated losing too. He would eventually become an NAIA All-American sprinter at Bethel College where he set numerous school records in the sprint events.

Rod and I gave high-fives and laughed on the sidelines at Geoff's pee-wee football games. He developed into an unstoppable running back. The quarterback would hand him the ball, he'd make a cut, and away he would go to the end zone. As a youngster, his natural speed helped him qualify for the Junior Olympics as a 200-meter sprinter several summers.

By the time he reached high school, he had become a three-sport star playing varsity football, basketball, and track. While his speed would be the ticket to college, he excelled as a fantastic basketball and football player. As I embarked upon a comeback from Legionnaire's disease in winter 2001, Geoffrey's high school basketball team made a solid run to the 2A State High School finals.

Famed ESPN college basketball commentator Dick Vitale colorfully describes young talented basketball players as "diaper dandies" and three point shots as "trifectas." Geoffrey and his best friend of many years, AJ, were sophomore diaper dandies. They both played a key role in Harding High defeating Batesville High 73–70 at Conseco Fieldhouse in downtown Indianapolis for the 2001 2A Indiana State Basketball Championship. AJ's dad, Al Gooden, a longtime friend of mine from high school and a wonderful basketball player in his day, coached Harding's basketball team. "Big Al" inserted both AJ and Geoffrey in the game to give the starters rest and a spark on offense. My mind drifted back to the days in my basement watching them play ball and later serving as ball boys for Harding's basketball team.

They both came through big-time with stifling back-court defense and scoring at key junctures. Geoffrey made two "trifectas" in the first half, forcing Batesville to abandon its 2–3 zone defense for standard man-to-man defense, swinging the individual match-up advantage to the Hawks who were bigger and more physical than the boys from Batesville. By halftime, the Hawks powered their way to a ten-point lead. Although Batesville clawed its way back into the game and took a one-point lead with thirty seconds remaining, the Hawks prevailed. For the first time in twenty-seven years, a Fort Wayne high school had won a state basketball championship.

My pride brimmed. I found myself in the stands of Conseco Fieldhouse overwhelmed and crying tears of joy as I watched my baby and his team cut down the nets, receive medals, and hoist the championship trophy. I may have missed this special moment had not Geoffrey and his sister taken care of me in my small Houston apartment just a few months prior.

I busily worked on completing my own personal trifecta during these days. I had heard about the 175-mile, two-day, MS 150 bike tour a couple months before Geoff's championship run. This would be the ultimate challenge to prove my recovery neared completion. My company sponsored a team of riders. I wanted to represent my company.

This Houston-to-Austin bike tour to benefit multiple sclerosis research was the largest biking event in the country. It would take nine thousand riders ninety-five miles on day one, along the beautiful Texas Hill Country to LaGrange, Texas, for an overnight stay at Fayette County Fairgrounds. The Fairgrounds is a huge fifty-acre park that becomes a tent city with individual and corporate tents sprawled as far as the eye can see to accommodate the riders' overnight stay. Saturday afternoon and evening featured a big party with bands, food, and drinks for the riders. It became a time of fellowship and camaraderie for cyclists from all over the world, their families, and friends.

My company provided a tent, food, and drinks for its twenty-plus riders. "The Company," as I affectionately referred to it, had come up big in my book. We had several volunteers who served food and drinks and made us comfortable. Tina and Martha, who both worked in my call center, made me proud because they volunteered to help that weekend. They drove from check point to check point both days to cheer riders and helped however they could. Our team captain Mark and his girlfriend Edith were the most unselfish people I had met in a long time. Even though they were exhausted from the long ride, they were constantly checking on everyone else. Mark had heard my story and paid special attention to make sure I held up during the ride and at the campsite.

Sunday morning, we woke up to a pancake breakfast and then lined up for a 7 am start, leaving LaGrange and finishing some eighty miles later in Austin. The ride had everything to do with the generosity of the human spirit and overcoming mind-boggling odds, and in the end, the focus of the tour centered on the efforts to raise money for research and finding a cure for multiple sclerosis. This event had a special meaning for me besides proving that I could complete my personal trifecta of running, biking, and returning to work full-time.

One of my close friends and neighbors, Chris, had multiple sclerosis. I loved Chris. We were prayer partners and went to the same church in Fort Wayne. My love extended to his wife Pam and their children, Abigail and Tim. Pam never knew she was one of my heroes. She had an unwavering faith. She had enough strength to support the entire family. Chris really couldn't care for himself, so Pam did everything. She dressed, fed, groomed, bathed, and handled him mostly by herself. She also took care of their kids, their modest home, and worked outside of the home. The woman was a saint.

No one had more faith than Chris. By the time I met him in the early 1990s, he couldn't walk. I used to laugh when I saw him buzzing all over the place in his electric wheelchairs and carts. He would race his children and act like a big kid, playing demolition derby. I saw him ride his cart almost a mile to the neighborhood elementary school for PTA meetings or other events.

Pam would take him to church. If Chris saw me in the common areas, he would bump into me with his cart and giggle. I'd punch him hard and hop out of the way. He always tried to get in the last lick. One fall, our church had a men's retreat weekend at a camp north of Fort Wayne. I enjoyed the honor and privilege of taking Chris with me, caring for him, and spending the weekend with him. Our hearts were knitted together that weekend. Caring for him wasn't easy, and I gained a measure of respect for what Pam had to endure day in and day out.

Even though I shared a lot of hilarious moments with Chris, it wasn't all jokes and fun. From time to time, I walked the half block to his house so we could talk about scripture and pray. These times served as equivalents of boys' night out for Chris and a much-needed respite for Pam. She would leave us boys alone to spend much-deserved time alone. Sometimes cookies or muffins would make an appearance. Since we were there alone, Chris and I munched like the hungry boys we were.

"What can I pray for this week, my friend?"

The answer never changed. "Cal, I want to walk again. I want to run and play with Tim and Abigail."

"Okay. Let's believe God for a healing." I would pray for Chris and hold his hand tight and then he would pray for me. My problems and challenges always seemed so small when I really got serious and let my mind come to grips with what Chris and his family were dealing with.

I prayed and believed. Chris never recovered. He never walked again. I was devastated when he died, but I tried to keep a stiff upper lip. I had survived my struggle with Legionnaire's disease, but Chris had lost his battle. He was a much better man than me. I hadn't been the best husband or father because I spent too much time and energy trying to climb the corporate ladder, watching women, and impressing people who probably really didn't care about me at all. Chris lived his life confined to a wheelchair, but he had not checked out on his family. Even when the MS got so bad it took away his ability to speak, he still had a smile for me and everyone else. No one knew that inside my head, I had a nagging question that wouldn't go away. I couldn't figure out why he died and I lived.

I flew to Indiana for his funeral not long before the MS 150. His funeral was a celebration. Pam's courage and strength inspired many. Everyone had stories about his antics and teasing. I also had my private memories of sitting with him and praying that God would reverse the terrible effects of MS. I believed Chris found his peace. I knew in my spirit he lived in heaven and ran all over the place just having a blast until we got there with him. Heck, he probably biked in heaven too.

I thought about him for the first thirty miles or so getting out of Houston during the MS 150. The first few miles came easily. The terrain was relatively flat. Around Houston, a person could stand on a beer can and see all the way to Dallas. Things changed quickly though as we moved on and approached towns northwest of Houston. Although the Texas hill country is breathtaking during the spring with bluebonnets and other natural flora and fauna, the ride is ultimately two days of spirit-breaking hills and headwinds across several counties. The most challenging portion of the ride is during day two as riders pedal through a beautiful state park. The hills are steep and the road is narrow. Crashes are common as determined bikers navigate their way through the park. This all pushed me to the very brink of quitting but for one thing.

During registration, the race sponsors provided orange bandanas to riders to commemorate the lives of those stricken with MS. I got a black marker and wrote on my bandana:

"I'm riding for my friend Chris Fulton."

I tied the bandana to my handle bars and kept it there the entire 175 miles. Every time a hill seemed too steep to climb, my legs felt like heavy tree trunks or the wind pushed against my tall frame with vigor, I'd look down at the bandana, and think about my friend. Chris helped me power over hill after hill all the way to Austin. I forgot all about Legionnaire's disease more than a few times during the tour, thanks to my friend and prayer partner. His spirit was with me that weekend.

In March I had returned to the office full-time without much fanfare at all. It had become a small step in the recovery process. With running and biking conquered, I had scored the trifecta of a lifetime.

Chapter 24
A REAL 2001 ODYSSEY

Dealing with Depression

BY ALL ACCOUNTS, I COULD BE considered a walking miracle. I'd conquered running, biking, and driving. I had returned to work. The struggles inside my head were a different matter altogether. It was one thing being physically gifted enough to rely on muscle memory to accomplish the impossible, but quite another to have a silent curve ball thrown at one's mental and spiritual psyche. Try as I might to accept the losses in my life, I couldn't seem to get over the fact that the "old" Cal had disappeared forever.

Was I really "never better"? Never better, because I'd driven a car virtually the width of the country? Never better, because I had run a half marathon? Never better, because I rode a bicycle between cities and over every hill in Southern Texas? Maybe, but life held much more for me than tackling those physical feats. My makeup included a complex multifaceted composition of mind, body, soul, and spirit. I worked on overcoming physical frailties. I still tried very hard to hit the silent mental curve ball that rocked my invisible world.

One day, I'd be upbeat and on top of the world. The next day, I'd be weepy and sad. There were days in my office in which I'd turn my back from the door to hide tears after listening to my prized role-play cassette. I'd pull the word list out of my back pocket and stare at it through tears wondering if I'd ever be able to speak normally again.

I suffered from the grief of losing the part of my persona that came with being a quick-witted talker. Despite all the spiritual professions to others that I had found true contentment in just being alive, I still secretly struggled with the lost opportunity to continue the climb up the corporate ladder. In addition, I felt guilty, because although I lived and had achieved some miraculous milestones, I had returned to constantly questioning God about my plight. My brain spun a scrambled concoction. Why had this happened?

No one knew the pain I felt inside because I tried my best to hide it. Even when I went to my church, I never talked to anyone or tried to interact in any small group activity. It's easy to get lost in a megachurch. I listened to the music and the speakers and then drove home. The depression lurked there, waiting, always waiting.

I found myself withdrawing from people once I left work. During the day, I could easily hide in my office in virtual isolation. Lois kept my gate. I could schedule staff meetings at my discretion. The other members of the senior team worked twenty-five miles away, so I didn't have to worry about interacting with them except via e-mail.

Michele tried her best to help me. She cared for me, fully understanding I dealt with a natural grieving process. I had no idea that is what I faced. She had experienced the grief of losing a child, and had witnessed other heart-wrenching situations. These experiences provided her with special insights. Before moving to Houston, she worked in a Grand Rapids hospital as an assistant in an obstetrics special care program. Her job entailed helping underprivileged mothers and families having difficulties with achieving full-term pregnancy. In that role, she managed over forty volunteers who assisted women during pregnancy and the recuperative period following delivery. One of the primary thrusts of the program provided expectant mothers with training and tools to ensure adequate birth weights.

During her stint at this job, she worked with several high-risk pregnancy mothers who lost babies due to failed in-vitro fertilization, early labor episodes, or complications with multiple fetuses. The case that touched her heart the most involved a sixteen-year-old mother carrying her second child. One evening during the third trimester of the pregnancy, the young mother experienced complications when her water broke prematurely. She rushed to the hospital but was ultimately turned away because she had no insurance. This nearly became a death sentence for both mother and child. The girl developed infection and went into full respiratory arrest. Her organs started to shut down, all of her toes were amputated and she slipped into a ninety-day coma.

Miraculously, the baby delivered in perfect health. Once the young mother regained consciousness and recovered, Michele sprang to action by working countless hours to help get assistance for both mother and children. She tried everything within her power to help this girl succeed, including helping her return to school.

Now the time came for another restoration project with her beloved Cal. Michele had heard my story of being sick but yet turned away at the emergency room with no treatment. While I had not lost a baby, I had lost the old Cal. The parallels were compelling to her. She tried to help me get my confidence back and grow more comfortable with the new Cal. Her goals included pushing me to become fully independent. I had the same goal.

It wasn't working all that well. The fault belonged to me. There were times I'd take two steps forward only to take three steps back in handling the mental challenges of the Legionnaire's experience. I was prone to daily pity parties when I thought about my "old" self. My emotions were raw. Crying over the simplest event became a daily occurrence. Through it all, Michele would lovingly encourage me to look forward.

"I like *this* Cal. I really didn't know the other Cal all that well. He's gone now. I love this Cal. Baby, you have to move on."

"I...know...you...are...right."

Even though our relationship felt special and symbiotic, the scale tipped solidly in my direction in terms of neediness. I smothered her and did not make the steps to get mentally healthy on my own. It became too much to deal with for two people without a lot of history between them. By late spring, we went separate ways and did not see each other again for a full year.

All the while, Doc had seen and heard my struggles. She had been praying for me. She believed God could heal my mind just as he had given me the strength to compete in and complete challenging physical events. She encouraged me to search scriptures and pray for God's peace in my life.

In addition to taking spiritual medicine, I also needed to take the steps to get professional help. This fact seemed hard to for me to grasp, accept and to initiate even though I experienced some classic symptoms of depression. For me they included:

- Constant sadness about lost ability to communicate effectively
- Hopelessness that I could ever regain my "polish"
- Trouble sleeping (lucky to get four or five hours sleep each night)
- Low energy and fatigue (sometimes I felt like a dirty washcloth lying in a corner)
- Feeling worthless or guilty for questioning God

Try as I might, I could not shake any of these problems.

Overcoming the issues proved difficult, in part, because I saw getting professional help as a sign of weakness. I feared if people at work—especially the executive managers—found out I took medication or attended therapy sessions, they would think I was unfit for the job or too emotional to lead a large organization. The other thought that stopped me was a ridiculous notion that black people don't go for therapy or take antidepressants. An impromptu meeting with a colleague changed all of that for me.

After a summer staff meeting at the downtown campus, I stopped by HR to visit with my director friend, Tina. We had built a great rapport because of our Hoosier upbringing. We teased each other big-time. She had been very helpful to my family during the darkest days the previous fall as I began recovery. She answered all the questions about my pay and benefits and kept in close contact with us.

This day should have been nothing more than an exchange of pleasantries and the obligatory teasing. We got through that, and then Tina looked me square in the eye.

"So, Cal, how are you really doing these days?"

The flood gates opened. Before I knew it, tears were falling and I babbled uncontrollably. Everything came out: missing my kids, not being able to speak clearly, the failed marriage, being sad all the time, fatigue, my scrambled brain, memory loss, and not being able to run fast anymore. I poured out everything to Tina. This very personal stuff had left me sad and broken.

While I cried my eyes out and emptied my soul, Tina listened quietly and let me get it all out. Then she offered help and advice that would start to move my life in a different direction.

"Have you talked to anyone about this, Cal?"

"No. Not...real...ly." I sobbed right there in her office. Good thing we were behind closed doors.

"You need to." She handed me a brochure. "This Employee Assistant Program is available to all employees. One of the EAP features is three free counseling sessions. You can find someone either close to work or your home. The company will cover the cost."

I agreed to make the call.

A few days later, nearly the same scene played out at a visit with Dr. Tiwari. It was supposed to be a routine follow-up visit. It started out that way. She conducted the same examination I'd had with her the last couple visits.

"Touch your right finger to your nose like this. Now, your left."

This got easier every time I saw her.

"Follow my finger with your eyes."

Her finger moved across my face from left to right, and my eyes followed her finger without any effort at all. The obligatory tap on my knees, shins and heels with a soft mallet followed. My limbs must have moved correctly, because she smiled.

"Now, walk over there and back."

I still had to take my time and concentrate when I walked, but I had gotten better and better at walking straight and keeping my balance. Walking started to become a piece of cake, because I'd been working out with regularity.

"Good, Mr. King. How have you been feeling?'"

"Kinda...tired...I...am...still...hav...ing...a...real...hard...time...

talk...ing. I...have...been...run...ning...and...biking...but...I...can't...
stand...up...and...ped...al."

She nodded and waited, to give me all the time I needed. I think Dr.
Tiwari knew I was looking better but had some things going on in my
head.

"It's...been...so...hard." The tears started. I hated to break down in front
of this pretty woman, but none of the male bravado crap mattered now.

"Don't worry, Mr. King."

"I...just...want...to...be...my...old...self...a...gain...Peo...ple...look...
at...me...fun...ny." More tears. "I...th—th—thought...I...would...be...
all...bet...ter...by...now.

The tears gave away to sobbing. Dr. Tiwari put her hand on my shoulder.
It was a comforting touch. It made me think of Michele. I missed her so
much.

"I think you're experiencing some depression. It's not surprising given
what you've been through. I'm going to prescribe something to help you."

I tried to gather myself, and I pulled out a hanky to blow my nose and
wipe the tears away. "I...have...to...work...so...I...hope...this...medi...
cine...won't...keep...me...from.....do...ing...my...job. Will...it?"

The stories about people flatlining on antidepressants came to mind. I had
no desire to be a zombie, but I hurt inside. I felt exhausted behind this whole
mental game. So, if this stuff would work, I'd give it a try.

"No. It will help you with the highs and lows. It will smooth them out
and will help you deal with some of these issues more easily."

I put all the crap about the stigma that comes with taking antidepressants
behind me. At this point, I didn't care what other people thought. I desperately
needed help and started taking the medicine she prescribed the same day.

"I'll...do...it." That's what I had promised Tina earlier. Although I had
to psyche myself up to do so, I kept my word. I called the confidential help
line and emptied my heart to a voice over the phone. I didn't hear a message
saying the call would be taped or monitored for quality assurance. That gave
me some solace. No one would play the tape and snicker at my broken speech
and pathetic problems. The phone counselor shared the name of a therapist
in Bellaire, the neighborhood adjacent to mine. A few days later, after a full
day of work, I met Sharon in her office.

My deodorant stopped working, and sweat trickled down my forehead as
I rode the elevator up to meet with her. No one lingered on the floor or waited
in her waiting room. It seemed as if the whole building had been deserted,
even though virtually every space in the parking lot had been taken. This
pleased me, because I didn't want to see anyone, and I didn't want anyone
to see me.

A tall, middle-aged woman with a twinkle in her eye and a peaceful smile greeted me.

"Hi, you must be Cal. I'm Sharon. Come in and make yourself comfortable."

Her voice was laced with a graceful East Texas tone similar to Lois's. Her tone said "Hi friend, come in and relax a while." Her easy-going style indeed instantly comforted me. The office provided a place of comfort, and she made it easy to share my feelings. She listened intently, took notes, and asked leading questions. I never saw "the Look" or sensed any pity at all. This place provided a cocoon of mental safety.

The three free sessions were over before I knew it. I had only began to pour out my heart to Sharon and wasn't ready to stop. I had found a respite in her company. She was patient and kind.

"This is the end of the sessions supported by your company. Do you want to continue?"

"Yes...I...would." We arranged for more meetings. Each week I looked forward to the going to this place where I could be brutally honest about my inner most thoughts. There was no judgment, just a listening ear. She made a proposal that I didn't see coming at all.

"I'd like you to participate in a group."

"What...is...th—th—that?"

"It's a weekly meeting with several people in which you all share experiences and work together toward solutions."

I'd seen this on television. Those sessions were for crazy people. I wasn't crazy and didn't need this. Sharon saw me struggling, but she didn't intervene. It was as if she knew I had to work through his concept. I wasn't thrilled about the idea, but I trusted Sharon, so I agreed.

It was a big step. I had been avoiding social gathering as much as I could, because I felt totally ashamed of how I sounded. I had even gone as far as taking lessons in American Sign Language at a local church so I could communicate effectively that way. I had faked being hearing impaired at service counters and other places to justify "the Look." It had dawned on me that that charade really wasn't funny at all. Learning ASL might be a useful thing to learn, not because I wanted to fake a disability, but because it could be an effective means of communication. Now I would be sharing my thoughts with complete strangers though my own dysarthria-laden speech.

The cool thing about being in group was that we had all signed confidentiality agreements. I had seen plenty of those during my business career. What the agreements said is that we agreed not to share the names of people in our group. We further agreed not to share what was discussed in our sessions with anyone outside of our group. Group sessions, like the one-on-ones with Sharon, were a completely safe venue to share our innermost thoughts.

The conversations would have made fantastic material for a book or movie. My group mates were from the entire continuum of socioeconomic backgrounds. There were males and females. We all had one thing in common: all of us had a tough problem to overcome, and we were determined to attain that goal.

Attending group therapy became one of the best decisions I had ever made. Sharon facilitated masterfully. She stepped in only when she absolutely had to. For the most part, we controlled the flow of conversations. Our discussions, even though sometimes spirited, were extremely helpful to one another. We challenged each other and consoled one another. We also helped each other work through events as they arose. I had my share of them that were worth talking about.

Earlier that year at her retirement party, Doc mentioned her dream that we all go visit her childhood home during the upcoming summer. I'm fairly certain the gift I presented her inspired this dream. In late August, her dream had come true. Doc, my siblings, their spouses, and all their children piled in a huge van and drove from Indiana to Memphis. I flew in from Houston, and the gang picked me up at the airport.

"Cashflow!" Linda ran to me when she spotted me. She hugged me so tight, I thought my lungs would explode. One by one, they all got their hugs. Over the hot summer, I had found myself getting calmer and a more comfortable with the new Cal. Dr. Tiwari had been absolutely right about the medicine she prescribed. It smoothed out the highs and lows of my emotions. The group sessions helped me work through my sadness and sense of loss. I started to flatline. I hadn't realized that up until this point. While I was excited to see my family, I couldn't believe how calm I was.

I hadn't told my family or friends that I used therapy or antidepressant drugs. A mother always knows her child. Doc's instincts told her there was something different about me since she'd seen me a couple months before. After we checked into our hotel, Doc zoomed in on me. Linda, Rod, and Carla were all in the room, so it I thought it made sense to get this over with once and for all.

"CK, you seem so calm and not as sad as the last time I saw you. What's going on with you?"

"Mom...I...am...taking...medi...cine...that...helps...me...deal... with...some...of...the...prob...lems...I...am...hav...ing...with...my... re... cov...ery."

"What are you taking?"

"Celexa. I...am...al...so...do...ing...th—th—thera...py." I felt better once I got that out on the table. Everyone seemed to think those were good moves, although Doc did have some concerns based on years of working with patients using antidepressants over long periods of time.

"I just don't want you to be zoned out. You have to be careful with some of that stuff. There are side effects."

All I knew is that I had started to really get a handle on things mentally. I was determined to keep taking my medicine and going to group no matter what anyone said. So I listened to my mom's concerns, but my mind had already been made up. I would not stop either treatment.

We spent a long weekend and took in as many sights as we could in Memphis: the Peabody Hotel with its promenading ducks, the Lorraine Motel where Dr. Martin Luther King Jr. was assassinated, and a very fun evening on Beal Street listening to great music and enjoying the crowd. But the highlight of our visit was the day we spent in Frenchmans Bayou.

We visited mom's old church and the spot of her baptism. We drove all over town and to the site where my Gramps had built their home. Sadly, it was gone, as was Doc's original high school building. Just before we left Frenchmans, we drove by a well-kept home. A car parked in the driveway began to gently back out into the street. We waved and the gentleman driver returned the gesture.

Doc recognized the man. We pulled over to chat with him. It was the man she knew as "Rat" Speck. They exchanged pleasantries.

"Do you know who I am?" Doc said.

"Why, yes, you're Price Love's daughter." I raised my eyebrows. My sisters didn't seem to have a clue about the significance of this. Neither did Rod.

"I sure am. Let me introduce you to my children. Guys, this is Mr. Rat Speck."

He corrected her and shared his given name. I said hello as did my siblings. Everyone was cordial. My mind fell on all the stories Doc had shared with me. Even though I was flatlining, I felt an uncomfortable heat rise inside. "Where ya'll visiting from?"

"Indiana," we all said in unison.

"Well, good seeing you, we have to be on our way." Doc cut the visit short. I was glad she did. I wondered if he was one of the people who had sent word to my Gramps to tell my parents to get that "white" baby out of town.

"Ya'll take care, and have a safe trip home now."

We were on our way back to Memphis. We drove past the shiny new post office, and I made fun of Doc. Everyone laughed. The laughter turned to tears for some as the family dropped me off at the Memphis airport for my return flight to Houston. Incredibly, I wasn't one of the people crying, because my highs and lows were truly flattened.

I had learned to go through the flatlined motions of my life right up until the morning of September 11. That morning started off with me doing my daily early morning ritual of running, biking, pushups, and crunches. After my workout, I turned on the *Today Show* to listen to Matt Lauer and Katie Couric before leaving for work. Something felt different that morning. I had taken off my workout gear and was about to shower and dress. I walked into my living room to do the obligatory time check. Neither Matt nor Katie appeared on screen. The camera trained on the World Trade Center. One of the towers emitted smoke. I thought a small plane had veered off course and struck the tower. But as the minutes rolled by, I understood the gravity of the moment. A second plane had slammed into the twin tower. Then the reports started to pour in about another plane crashing into the Pentagon as well as a plane crash in southwest Pennsylvania.

In the days following September 11, many people were afraid to fly. I had flown back and forth from Indiana for over a year now with little regard for safety or security. I wasn't about to let this incident scare me out of flying. I had a special trip to make. My friend Scott had qualified for the upcoming Ironman Triathlon World Championship on October 6 in Kona, Hawaii. He found a place to stay for free for an entire week.

"Cal, you should come to Kona with me. My sister Brenda's brother-in-law lives there. He has a guesthouse with several beds. Dude, we could stay there the whole week for free."

"Really?"

"Yeah. It's no problem."

He didn't have to ask me twice. I had plenty of vacation time left and nothing going on. A chance to go to Hawaii, with only the expense of food and air fare, was too good to pass up. It was an opportunity to treat myself and revisit one of the most beautiful places on earth. This trip would be all about healing my mind in paradise, while hanging out with Scott and the friends he had made during various triathlon events. I booked my flight.

Scott was one of my all-time athletic heroes. He had qualified for the Ironman World Championship by completing a qualifying triathlon event in just over ten hours just six weeks before the championship triathlon. The gravity of swimming 2.4 miles, biking 112 miles, and finishing with running a full marathon (26.2 miles) was not lost on me. It was an incredible feat. I could barely finish a half marathon, let alone run another half, bike over a hundred miles, and swim over two miles on the same day!

The cool thing about Scott was, except for his finely chiseled body, you would have never known he was a world-class athlete. He never tried to overwhelm or impress anyone around him. He lived a down-to-earth regular life working out with his buddies. He wasn't stingy with workout or nutrition tips. More than once, he ran alongside me to help me qualify for the Boston Marathon. He helped me pick and outfit my first bike. That choice had worked out just fine. This was a way to show my appreciation for what he had done for me over the years.

After one long ride with the Tri-Fudds, he told me, "You've taken to the bike real well, Calvin." He had taught many of us how to improve our riding skills. We all listened closely because the guy could ride like the wind. Scott had a $4,800 bike that looked like a *Star Wars* vehicle. We called it the "Wonder Bike."

When he registered and checked in Wonder Bike for the Ironman the day before the race, I stood in line with him. I had never seen so many super-fit human specimens in all my life. There were over 1,500 participants. The field of competitors hailed from over forty countries and nearly every state in the United States. All of them had very little body fat and very strong-looking legs, especially their calf muscles.

What a fantastic week of going to the beach, going for runs, and enjoying the Hawaiian sunsets. I hung out with Scott, his friend Steve from Twisp, Washington, our roommate for the week and fellow Ironman competitor. This time of total relaxation worked wonders for my mental health and became the culminating crown jewel of several months of searching for peace. The trade winds, breathtaking Hawaiian sunsets, megafit people, and the blue water substituted several weeks of group therapy sessions. I couldn't wait until that Saturday morning to experience this spectacle. I felt as excited as Scott and Steve did about the big day.

The Ironman race started at 7 am with a huge cannon blast on Kailua-Kona Bay. Scott and his 1,500 friends looked like ants thrashing about in the bay swimming a 2.4 mile rectangle. One by one, swimmers emerged dripping wet. They transitioned to their individual wonder bikes to embark on the 112-mile ride across the Hawaiian lava desert to Hawi and back. Once the bike portion of the race was completed, they ran a marathon all along the coast.

I walked the streets of Kona the whole day trying to catch glimpses of Scott as he finished the swim and bike stages of the race. I cheered for him as he neared town toward the end of the marathon and toward the finish line. At the end of the day, I felt spent and my feet ached from walking around in the tropical sun literally all day. I couldn't begin to imagine how tired Scott and all the other competitors must have been. He had a tough day as he finished in a tad over thirteen hours. The time didn't matter. He finished. This event provided the true and ultimate test of endurance and mind over matter. In my opinion, everyone who competed that day had become more than a winner. Their accomplishment inspired awe. Being there to celebrate with my friend meant a special honor for me. It became my way of thanking him for his friendship over the years.

October gave way to November, and November gave way to the Christmas holiday season. It was a time of reflection of a long, challenging year. Kathleen gave a special gift to all of her direct reports that year. The heart-shaped ornament, adorned with the stars and stripes of the American flag, captured my attention. A little folded card attached to the ornament with the words "Brave Heart" on the outside contained a typed message. The ornament was designed by Christopher Radko, commemorating September 11, 2001, and benefiting the American Red Cross. The card's message said:

"In the aftermath of the tragedies that took place September 11, 2001, the courage and resolve of the people of New York City, Washington, D.C., and southwest Pennsylvania—and every citizen of the free world—have been profoundly tested. Together we will pass this test...pass with the flying colors of the flag shown in the ornament I call Brave Heart.

I have designated my net profits from Brave Heart to the disaster relief fund of the American Red Cross in Greater New York. Many retailers across the country have agreed to donate their own proceeds from the purchase to local Red Cross chapters.

Thank you for joining us in support of the brave hearts whose heroism inspires us all."

The gift fit, given the mood of our country post-9/11. Kathleen also gave each one of her team members a personalized message in a Christmas card. The simple note she wrote inspired and encouraged me:

December 2001

Dear Cal,
You are the "bravest heart" on the team. I have learned so much from your determination, perseverance, and confrontation of your health and personal challenges. You are truly a leader and a survivor. You are wise, and you have the gift of vision—seeing how things could be better or different. Hang in there, my friend and colleague, the best is yet to come. Best wishes for a happy, healthy, peaceful, and prosperous 2002.

Kathleen

My odyssey year neared an end. I had lived through the hardest time in my life and passed my own tests—physical, spiritual, and mental. I learned lessons that fundamentally changed the way I thought about my life and the way I thought about others. I had started to get more and more comfortable just being myself, not worrying about the loss of the old Cal. In my "brave heart," I discovered that getting comfortable with the new me was one of the lessons God had been trying to teach me all along. It made enduring the 2001 odyssey more doable and the years to come more fulfilling and meaningful.

Epilogue

When my HR friend Tina asked me what the most difficult challenge for call center executives was, I immediately said "turnover." On the surface, the work of a call center customer service representative seems easy. Take calls, answer questions, provide guidance, solve issues, and then go home. There's much more to it. It's a daunting job even on a good day. Many CSRs simply get burned out from long hours of handling call after call, ungrateful callers, or a poor work environment. They move on, causing turnover of staff. Because of this staff turnover, call center managers are always recruiting and training new talent.

To prepare CSRs for the gauntlet of handling thousands of calls each month, most companies have a formalized multiweek training program. Because we always had strong trainers and excellent skill at selecting talent, very rarely did a new hire fail to complete training. The CSRs we hired were battle-tested and ready to face handling thousands of calls by the time they completed training.

I learned from watching class after class graduate and seeing people go from being "newbies" to true call center professionals. Some would go on to other roles within the company. When I started at my company in February 2000, class nineteen neared its graduation from training. After my Legionnaire's disease experience, I had the blessing and good fortune to witness many more classes of CSRs graduate during the next several years. I celebrated with class fifty and even class eighty-five. The classes just kept rolling along, and so did I.

Once I returned to work in 2001, I began a ritual with each new hire class that I continued in the years that followed. With each class, I would kick the trainers out of the room after the graduation ceremony and then spend an hour or so with the new CSRs. I claimed this as my time to share my story, answer any questions about the company, department, or the job, and then leave them with a word of encouragement for the challenges ahead.

I always paused for a minute to size up the group. In every class, there were sharp go-getters while others might not make it on the floor, even though we prepared them well. Most of the time, I could pick out the stars by body language and eye contact; I also knew the ones who wouldn't make it using the same instincts. I often remembered that Mr. Eckrich had decided I had "it" and decided to help me change my life forever.

Over the years, my success rate in picking winners and losers proved uncanny. Either someone had "it," which would make a difference on the floor, or they didn't. I hoped my speech would fire up the group and help everyone succeed. At the very least, new hires would learn about the culture and history of the department, as well as my philosophy about what we were trying to accomplish as we administered service to stakeholders.

The speech was always the same. I knew it by heart. I owned this opportunity to share the life lessons I had learned post August 2000. As the years went by, even though the effects of dysarthria lingered, I began to speak better. After three or four years, I could almost get words out shortly after I thought them. My brain had rewired itself just as Dr. Tiwari predicted.

Another reason for the improvement in speaking was the work of a great orthodontist. His skill in widening my bite, and my enduring the 840 days of pain, agony, and challenges of wearing braces gave my tongue more room to move and get stronger. The wider bite helped me with enunciation and basic linguistics. Therefore, my speech improved significantly. In addition, I gained the added benefit of improvement to my smile. All that helped well enough for me to get comfortable with public speaking again. It wasn't the same silver-tongued, silky flow, but I could hold my own and get my points across.

Addressing a class of "newbies" was fun because my story inspired people on so many different levels, within the confines of a setting in which I could exercise complete control. Most of the time, I'd take off my suit coat or sport jacket, sit on the edge of the small table in the front of a conference room, and address the new team seated at the U-shaped group of tables. Normally, one of the trainers would provide a very nice introduction. I'd smile, thank them, and then get to it.

"Hi, everyone. I'm Cal. As you've heard, I'm the vice president of operations with day to day responsibility for this call center site. I'm excited to meet all of you, and I congratulate you on your accomplishments. The fact that you're seated around the table tells me that you are very talented. I can share with you that normally managers interview up to ten people to find the one special person they are looking for, so this must be a very special group. I've heard good things about you from the training team. I welcome all of you on behalf of the management group and the officers here, and I look forward to getting to know each and every one of you as we begin working together."

Occasionally, I would look around and see "the Look" once I opened my mouth. Years of therapy and spiritual growth helped me overcome the hurt I used to feel when I saw it. Now, it was my job to help people understand disability and get comfortable with it. One of the life lessons I had learned was many people are uncomfortable with encountering those with impairment. This manifested itself through withdrawal, avoidance, pity, nervousness, or in some disgusting instances, cruel joking. I had learned my lesson well. Never make fun of someone who is not "normal." You never know what they have been through. Many are brave and more determined than anyone can ever understand.

"Before I continue, I need to share a story with you. You may have noticed that I have some difficulty speaking. I sound as though I'm hearing impaired."

I pointed to my ears.

"I hear very well. So let me tell you what's going on with me, so you can get comfortable and we can move on. I joined the company in February of 2000, having come here from Indiana where I ran a call center for one of our competitors, Lincoln Life. How many of you are from Houston?"

A few hands would go up.

"Let me tell you, I love it here. I came down to interview right after Y2K. Ya'll remember the Y2K hoopla, don't you? Anyway, when I boarded the plane in Indiana, it was minus ten degrees, and there were ten inches of snow on the ground. A couple hours later, I got off the plane at George Bush airport. It was seventy degrees, and there wasn't cloud in the sky. I called my mom and said, 'I'm moving to Texas's even before I had interviewed with anyone!'"

People smiled and nodded. Some had lived north of the Mason-Dixon Line and knew all about the "Hawk."

"Things were going well here. We initiated some new strategies and started to build the infrastructure we have today. In August of that year, I decided to attend a call center conference in Chicago with another VP. It was a wonderful time of networking and looking at cutting-edge call center technology. All-in-all, it was a great trip. I saw some old friends and enjoyed Chicago. When we returned, my friend was fine. I came back with Legionnaire's disease."

The new CSRs who were older and had heard of the disease gasped. They had heard or seen stories about the horrible outbreaks. Those who hadn't heard of it (usually the younger ones) looked puzzled.

"As some of you know, it's a rare disease that affects one's pulmonary functions and leads to pneumonia. It's a bacterial-based disease that hides in air conditioning systems or cooling towers."

I pointed to the dust covered vents in the ceiling.

"I thought I had the flu, but it got worse and worse. I developed a very high fever and nearly died.

"There was another problem for me. In very rare cases, this disease causes swelling of the cerebellum, which leads to speech and motor skill impairment. Unfortunately, I experienced that part of the disease. As a result, I have a condition called dysarthria, which is a slurring of the speech. The motor-skill impairment is call ataxia. I've had to learn to speak one syllable at a time as well as learn to walk and move normally again. It's been a long journey, but the great news is, I survived.

"Now you know why I sound like this. When I'm excited or nervous or when something makes me laugh, the words come out funny. I have thick skin about all this. It's funny to me now. You see, if I slur words now, it's because I'm a little nervous and excited about meeting you. So if I say something you don't understand, just stop me and say, 'Cal, slow down, I didn't get that.' I never take myself too seriously.

"The biggest problem for me was I didn't know who to sue, because we are not sure where I got it from!"

The Look would disappear, and there would be smiles, nods, or giggles. Over the years, that story brought some to tears. For most, it was an inspiring tale, and they gained comfort with a person who had overcome living with disability. It is a lesson everyone needs to learn and I took great pride in being a conduit for the message.

"You can understand now why I'm so passionate about this call center. I nearly gave my life trying to figure out how to make it better. All I know is, every day is a good day, because I'm alive and here. Now we've got that out of the way, let's move on.

"I'll share a little bit about myself, so you'll know how I got here. I've spent nearly thirty years in the financial services industry. My first job was in a commercial bank where eventually I worked as a small business loan officer, but I worked in virtually every area of the bank during my time there. Some of you have worked as customer service reps at a bank…I've been there!

"Then I moved on and worked as an investment analyst in the real estate section of the investment management division at Lincoln National Corp. I did commercial real estate investments such as luxury apartments, strip centers, warehouses, outlet malls, and office buildings like this one we work in. It was the coolest job I ever had. My territory was east of the Mississippi, so I got to travel to nearly every major city in the eastern United States.

"Next, by hook or crook, I ended up as an operations executive running back-office processing departments and the call center at Lincoln Life. When my boss at Lincoln left Indiana to come to American General, I followed her here to run this call center. I've been here ever since then."

I continued my discussion with a background of the company, department, and the management team. I wanted them to fully understand the rich and proud tradition of our call center and the company they were now a part of. Knowing history is important. I am grateful that Doc shared the story of my family. It gave me a sense of where I came from and who I belonged to. Knowing my history grounded me and helped me accept myself.

"Are you ready to hear my philosophy about customer service? It's really intense. Good thing you're sitting down. Are you sure you are ready?"

The crowd was much more relaxed then and ready to play along.

"Okay, here it comes…treat every caller as though you are talking to yourself, your mother, or your grandma! That's really deep, huh?"

The shrugs, groans, and giggles were well worth it. Everyone has heard of the Golden Rule. Most of the time, we are in too much of a hurry to practice it. All I tried to convey is what I had figured out. Always let the people God puts in your life know you think they are special and worth your time. Obviously CSRs can't get intimate with a strange voice over the phone, but there are real people that they interact with everyday that can be touched, helped, or inspired by a kind word or a gentle gesture. I tried to teach a valuable life lesson in the context of the workplace.

One of the ways I practiced this key learning was writing thank-you notes and letters. Periodically CSRs receive compliments from callers or the sales force. We made a practice of sharing those with the whole department by e-mail. I printed those announcements and wrote personal notes of appreciation and thanks to the CSRs and hand-delivered them to their workstations.

This simple act of saying thank you and recognizing exceptional service was beyond special to the recipient. On top of it, seeing the smiles on their faces did wonders for me. From time to time, CSRs would display these notes on their workstations. The very talented ones received so many notes from me over the years, they couldn't post them all. I wanted the staff to know I didn't take them for granted.

This learning carried over to my personal life. If I thought of a friend or loved one, I wrote a letter and sent it by snail mail. If I was pushed for time, I sent an e-mail or text message. This proved to be a great way to stay connected and to tell those that were special that they mattered to me. It's a lost art that needs to be found again.

"Okay, now I'll share the secret of success that I share with every class. It's very simple, in fact, it's one word: relax."

I would literally see people exhale and calm down.

"Relax. So far there have been over seventy-five new hire classes. Virtually everyone who has gone through the training has made it. If they can do it, so can you. Remember, I told you that you are among the best and the brightest in the industry. So…relax!"

That is the message I shared with every new hire class.

"Before I open this up for your questions, let me share a few personal things. I love to run and ride my bike, although I'm over fifty and can't do either one fast anymore. I'm married and have six children.

"My oldest son is a career military man and has done tours in Bosnia and Iraq. I have a daughter who graduated from Purdue and is now a registered dietician and helps patients with diabetes. I have a son who graduated from Bethel College with a degree in youth ministry and adolescent behavior. He is a case manager in a group home for troubled youth. I don't cuss in front of him anymore."

That line always elicited a laugh. I was proud of Geoff, Kristi, and Darrell. They were all grown and were doing something in life that made a difference in the lives of people. I liked to think I had a hand in that. I had passed on a legacy of success and an anointing for service to others.

In fall 2002 Michele called me. She wanted to see how things were going. We hadn't spoken or seen each other in over year, so I was shocked to hear from her. She had gone through a tough 2001 too, having been part of a workforce reduction and navigating several jobs. She had a tough time providing for her boys but was doing the best she could. All in all, she got by and just wanted to reconnect with a friend who was dear to her. I understood the importance of making a reconnection.

I was thrilled to hear her voice and wanted to see her again. Things were different between us. I had learned to care for myself, and I had grown independent. I had gained a comfort with the new Cal and had become much more confident. I didn't need a caregiver anymore. I was looking for a life partner, and I had found her.

We began to date in earnest by Christmas and the following March we exchanged marriage vows before friends and a few family members. We started a wonderful life together and moved to the suburbs.

"I have a son who is a third-year college student and one who just graduated from high school and is serving in the military."

Michele's boys, Austin and Gregory, had grown up as teenagers in our home. I tried to father them and instill all the values I had learned over the years in them as if they were my very own. It had worked. They were fine young men.

"And I have a six-year-old daughter who has me totally wrapped around her adorable fingers!"

Not long after we were married, I found myself in a doctor's office with Michele listening to the results of an ultrasound.

"The baby looks fine. Her heartbeat is strong, and things are going well."

I couldn't believe I was going to have a new baby in my late forties after all I'd been through. While Michele and I shared the joy and celebration about this blessing, secretly I feared the worst. Would I pass along dysarthria and ataxia to this child? I explained my journey with Legionnaire's disease to the doctor. She assured us that that incident shouldn't affect the baby at all. My heart calmed. By the end of 2003 our baby girl was born, Lourdess Lynn, the miracle baby.

I'd learned that we all have God-given abilities and talents. It's more important to focus on and celebrate your abilities than to give importance to your disability. We can accomplish most anything we put our minds to. If I could overcome Legionnaire's disease and return to work, run a marathon and ride a bicycle from Houston to Austin, and overcome depression, watch out world, I could do anything. I could relax and just be myself no matter what episodes I faced in life. I had become comfortable with me. There had never been a better time than now because I was alive, talented, content, and well. I had found peace with my God and myself. It was easy to be a calming force in the lives of others and teach them to relax.